May 28, 1990, Choteau, Montana, U.S.A.

Dear Cheryl & Ted,

Just a mometo of your visit with us. Since you can't see all of Glacier Park this will help fill in what you missed.

With our love
Margeeto & Wilson
Irene & George

GLACIER COUNTRY

MONTANA'S GLACIER NATIONAL PARK

D1028801

NUMBER FOUR

MONTANA GEOGRAPHIC SERIES

Published By

MONTANA MAGAZINE, INC.

Helena, Montana 59604

Rick Graetz, Publisher
Mark Thompson, Editor
Carolyn Cunningham, Asst. Editor

1

GLACIER COUNTRY...

Grinnell Lake - Gordon Sullivan

Montana Magazine Inc., Publisher
Box 5630, Helena, MT 59604

ISBN 0-938314-05-X

MONTANA'S GLACIER NATIONAL PARK

Lake McDonald — Gordon Sullivan

Contents

About the Authors

Dave Alt is a professor in the Department of Geology, University of Montana. He is author of Roadside Geology of Montana and a recently completed college text. Dr. Alt writes a regular column about Montana's interesting geological history and features in Montana Magazine.

Curt W. Buchholtz teaches history at the Arapahoe Community College, Littleton, Colorado. He has worked seasonally in the park since the mid-'60s and has been published frequently on historical aspects of Glacier Park.

Bert Gildart is a freelance author specializing in outdoor subjects. He has completed book-length manuscripts for the National Park Service on Zion National Park, is author of Montana Wildlife, Number Three in the Montana Geographic Series, and is a regular contributor to Montana Magazine.

Bob Frauson retired from 30 years with the park service in 1982. He spent the last 20 years of his career as Hudson Bay District Ranger in Glacier National Park.

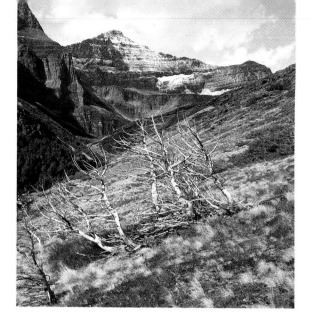

Siyeh Mountain. — Gordon Sullivan

Introduction

by Bert Gildart

Glacier National Park can be approached from all four points of the compass, but of the four the eastern approach is particularly inspiring. From this direction, as one travels Highway 2 through the flatlands of North Dakota and Montana, there is little hint of the vast mountainous range that looms ahead. Not until you are about 50 miles away and suddenly ascend from the depth of a deep coulee is there any real assurance that what appeared from the distance to be high glimmering clouds is in fact a lofty range of mountains shrouded in snow and ice.

Some two hundred and thirty years ago, when this range was first seen, adventurers were prompted to call this the "land of shining mountains." Today, this area could be called land of glorious adversity, for contemporary scientists tell us that the park was born of fire, quenched by torrential rains, inundated by vast seas, forced upward by by internal pressures, and then gouged by great continental ice sheets that came and went on at least four occasions. From this heritage, mountains were molded that reach up to touch the sky and cradle more than 200 lakes. Such is the legacy the eons left for some 60 mammals, 200 birds, and

1,200 plants that now inhabit the 1,538 square miles of Glacier National Park.

Glacier's features can be enjoyed in a number of ways. They can be enjoyed with drink in hand from a recliner on the terrace of one of the park's four magnificent lodges, on the deck of a launch or bus, by car, or by foot. Personal tastes determine how to spend available time, and so it is advisable to become acquainted with the park's generalized features as quickly as possible. The Park Service is prepared to assist in a number of ways.

Near each entrance is located either an information center or an elaborate visitor center. Here, rangers and naturalists are available to acquaint travelers with the various types of accommodations and interpretive programs offered by the park. In addition, displays have been arranged to assist interpretation and to guide the curious to places of interest.

At first encounter, the park may appear a forbidding place to explore, but this is not the case. It is bisected by the famed Going-To-The-Sun Highway, a road that provides motorists with numerous pullovers for an introduction to the park's various features. Or guided tour buses, provided by park concessioners, relieve motorists of driving.

After this introductory tour many visitors are inspired to take to foot. Almost 700 miles of trail await the hiker from low forested hills up to boulder-strewn passes. Along several of these trails, two back-country chalets are located that cater to hikers who do not want to carry heavy packs. In fact, it isn't necessary to tote anything more than bear bells, a toothbrush, camera, a canteen of water and map, as both Granite and Sperry chalets provide food and bedding.

There are remote campgrounds that provide hikers with nature's own accommodations. As in many other parks, these sites now require reservations made only in person at the park and on a first-come, first-serve basis.

Glacier is a park of incredible natural diversity. Five habitat types occur which are largely determined by weather, which in turn is influenced by altitude. In Glacier, then, it is possible to see inhabitants of the grassland, deciduous forest, coniferous forest, alpine tundra, and even the equivalent of polar ice and snow. To see the same types of zones elsewhere would require an extensive drive either north or south across the flatlands of the United States and Canada.

For those interested in learning about wildlife and the areas in which it can be found, it is advisa-

ble to learn Glacier's zones. In the spring, for instance, the initiated go to the coniferous forest to find elk, moose, squirrels and chipmunks, and the most cooperative and photogenic blue grouse. Here the bird's ventriloquistic hooting will direct those interested to its territory where it can be observed displaying its roseated shoulder patches and flaring out its eye patch as it warns other grouse away.

Perhaps Glacier's most spectacular of zones is the arctic-alpine. Here, hardy wildflowers have adapted to this harsh climate in a variety of ways. Some of the flowers are covered with fine hair-like structures which retard evaporation from the devastating winds. Other plants have overcome these forces by growing in matts and clumps. Almost all are perennials; the short alpine summer doesn't allow enough time for annuals to complete their cycle of life.

Despite the adverse conditions of the arctic-alpine zone, this area is home for some of the park's most interesting species of wildlife. Sheep may be seen in a variety of locales, but one particularly good spot is midway between Logan Pass and Granite Park Chalet. Interested visitors should leave Logan Pass and hike the Garden Wall Trail. Four miles later a huge formation will be reached that juts away from the main ridge of mountains like a flying buttress. This is Haystack Butte; here, in the bracing arch of this monolith, snow lingers and provides sheep as well as goats and marmots with a cool reprieve from the intense alpine sun. July through September is the best time to visit this area as with the advent of cool weather all but a few specially adapted species, such as the ptarmigan, either migrate from the arctic-alpine area, or hibernate beneath Glacier's inevitable mantle of winter snow.

Perhaps the following description of the park's geologic formation and its history will help you understand how Glacier Park came to be. The chapter called "Ranger's Notebook" is my attempt to anticipate for you the questions I was asked most frequently in 13 years as a seasonal ranger in Glacier. Finally, the editors have collected works here to give an overview of the kinds of plants and animals that inhabit the park.

This book is intended as an introduction to the general landscape, colorful past and natural diversity of the park many Americans think of first when they think of Montana and national parks.

Mount Wilbur from above Red Rock Lake — Gordon Sullivan

Geology:
Glaciated Park

Going-To-The-Sun Road at Logan Pass shows in this aerial view of Glacier's Peaks. — Mel Ruder

by Dave Alt

Glacier Park. It should have been called "Glaciated Park," because this is a poor place to see modern glaciers, and an excellent place to see mountains sculptured by the great ice-age glaciers. And an excellent place to see many other things.

Those mountains consist of sedimentary rocks more than one billion years old, some of the oldest well preserved sedimentary rocks in the country. The rocks preserve a record of the earth as it was before land plants existed, before there were animals of any kind, or atmospheric oxygen that animals might breathe. The record tells of a planet so unfamiliar that it might be another planet, as distant in space as in time.

So 60 million or so years ago, those rocks moved into their present position during the crustal movements that created the Rocky Mountains. Evidence of that movement is clearly visible in the landscape of the eastern part of Glacier Park.

During the last two or three million years, a succession of great ice ages brought enormous glaciers to North America and northern Europe, and high mountains all over the world. At least during the last ice age, and presumably during earlier ice ages, an ice cap covered the high areas of Glacier Park, and huge rivers of ice creaked awkwardly down the large canyons, scouring the bedrock and then dumping their load of eroded sediment farther down the valley.

The grinding rivers of ice melted about 10,000 years ago, leaving their legacy in the craggy peaks and ridges, the deep valleys, and the sparkling lakes that make the modern landscape of Glacier Park so magnificently beautiful. Only glaciation on a large scale can bring mountains to such rugged perfection.

First, a brief glance at the rocks.

The Archives of a Vanished Planet

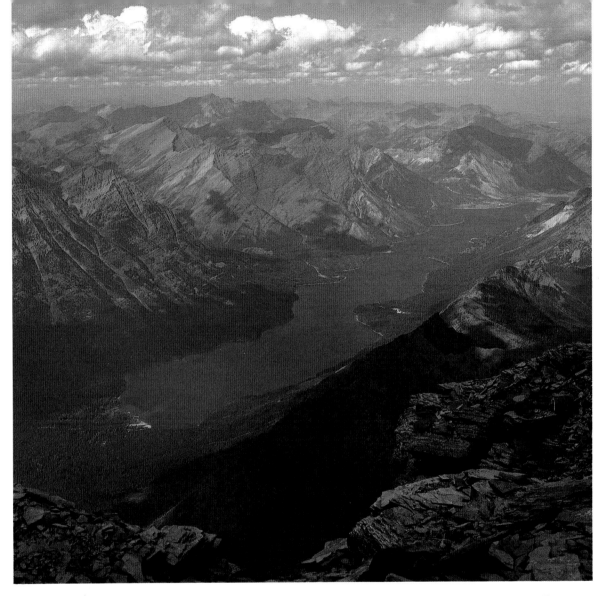

Waterton Lake from the summit of Mount Cleveland. Note how the glacially gouged Waterton Valley intersects smaller valleys, and recall that the lake itself is retained by moraine material deposited by the dying glacier thousands of years ago. — Bruce Selyem

Almost all the rocks exposed in the cliffs and roadcuts of Glacier Park began as layers of sand, mud, and lime mud deposited a billion or more years ago. Now they are layers of sandstone, mudstone and limestone. Most of the rocks in the park date from an extremely long interval that geologists call Precambrian time, because it preceded the Cambrian period when the first animals appeared on earth.

A billion years is a long time, even by the elongated standards of geology, and the Precambrian formations in Glacier Park rank among the oldest well-preserved sedimentary rocks in the country. Like all sedimentary rocks, they contain a record of the environment in which the original sand and mud accumulated. The Precambrian rocks in Glacier Park appear to have formed in an environment unlike any that exist today, unlike any that have existed for hundreds of millions of years. The earth of a billion years ago had not yet developed into the pleasant and hospitable home we know.

This is not the place to discuss the subject in detail, but it seems worth mentioning that billion-year-old sedimentary rocks commonly contain evidence of an atmosphere that contained only a trace of oxygen. We would quickly suffocate, if we could visit the earth of that time. Furthermore, the scarcity of atmospheric oxygen would have left the earth without its ozone layer, which now protects the surface from burning ultraviolet radiation.

However, the rocks do provide good reason to suspect that the Precambrian atmosphere did contain enormous amounts of carbon dioxide. Now we pass from the realm of solid observation into that of informed conjecture. If the ancient atmosphere did indeed include large amounts of carbon dioxide, that would have made the climate hot, because carbon dioxide causes a greenhouse effect. High temperatures, if they existed, would have increased the rate of evaporation from the oceans to create an effect that may have resembled a planetary sauna bath.

Picture then the shadeless landscape of Precambrian time. The barren land sweltered under heavy clouds, and was lifeless except for scummy growths of green algae in shallow pools of water. The seacoast lay somewhere near Glacier Park, probably shifting back and forth as the years passed. Most of the rocks we see in the park appear to have accumulated near that coast, some on land, others in shallow water not very far from land.

The rock formations of Glacier Park are few in number, very thick, and appear as broad bands of distinctive color in the landscape. Anyone can quickly learn to recognize them. Pebbles eroded from those formations make the brightly colorful stream beds that so many visitors to the park remember long after they forget some of the more spectacular sights.

The Altyn Limestone

The oldest Precambrian formation in Glacier Park is the Altyn limestone of the eastern mountain front. It tends to be a bit inconspicuous, even though it is about 2,000 feet thick, and is most easily seen around the Many Glacier Hotel and the east end of St. Mary Lake. Altyn limestone is almost white in fresh roadcuts, tan on weathered surfaces, and contains numerous sand grains and small pebbles. It appears to have accumulated in shallow waters, perhaps in sea water, although there is no way to be quite sure of that. The Altyn limestone passes upward into the green and dark green mudstones of the Appekuny formation.

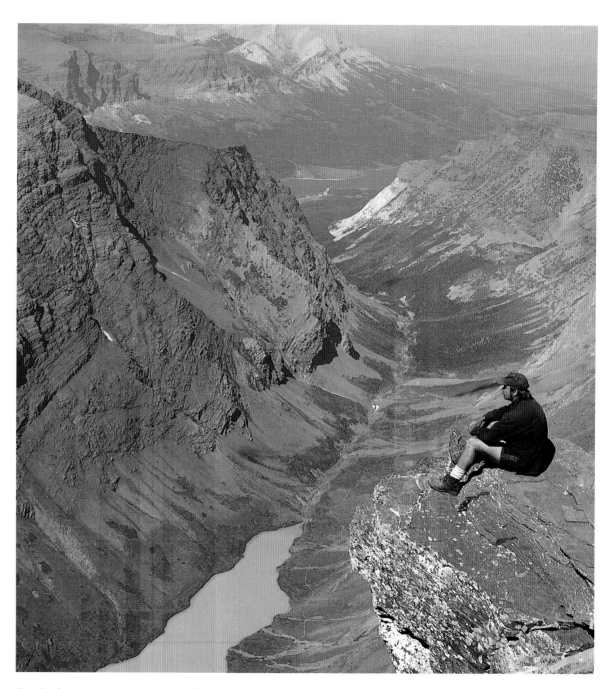

Track of glaciers past. View from Siyeh Mountain. Also notice the red band of Grinnell mudstone on the valley wall opposite the hiker. — Bruce Selyem

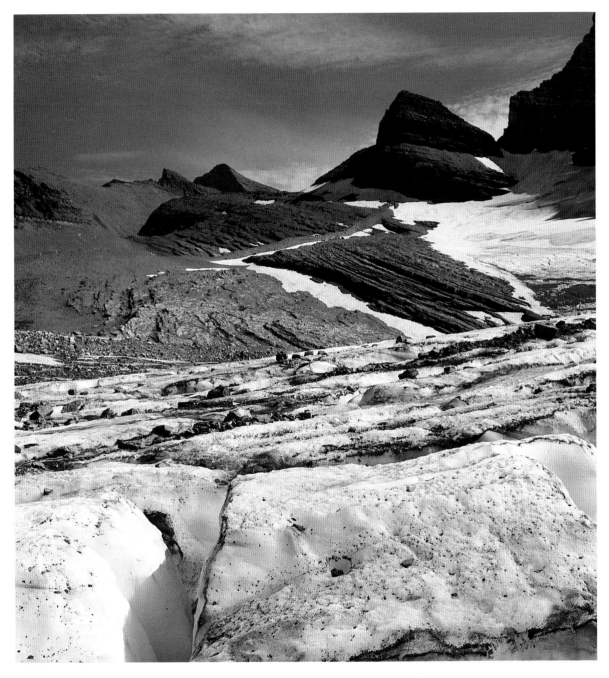

Grinnell Glacier carrying away its load of ice-plucked rock and debris. — Bert Gildart

The Appekuny Mudstone

The Appekuny mudstone is several thousand feet of somber green rock that becomes very dark in the western part of the park. The formation is more than 3,000 feet thick, and it forms a dark gray or greenish gray band in the landscape. At close range, it is simply layered green rock in the eastern part of the park, rock so dark that it is almost black in the western part. Any green rock in Glacier Park is almost certainly Appekuny mudstone.

At the top of the Appekuny mudstone, layers of red mudstone begin to appear, and they increase in number upwards. Geologists draw the contact between the Appekuny mudstone and the Grinnell mudstone above it where the red begins to overwhelm the green.

The Grinnell Mudstone

The Grinnell mudstone is about 2,500 feet thick, a broad reddish band in the landscape. Roadcuts of Grinnell mudstone are as red as a freshly painted barn, as they should be, because the same iron oxide pigment colors both. Except in the highest mountains near the middle of the park, any red rock in Glacier Park is likely to be Grinnell mudstone.

Watch the exposures of red mudstone for fossil mudcracks and ripple marks that look as though they were on a modern mudflat at low tide. Similar structures also exist in the green Appekuny formation, although not nearly so abundantly as in the red mudstones. As we look at those ripple marks and mudcracks, we see the remains of rippling pools of shallow water that lay here a billion years ago, and of mudflats that baked hard in the heat. However, geologists cannot be sure whether those pools and mudflats existed near the seashore, along the borders of a desert lake, or perhaps in some obsolete environment that has not existed since Precambrian time.

Both the Appekuny and Grinnell mudstones contain a few beds of white sandstone that make prominent ledges on the hillsides. Some of the most beautiful rock outcrops in the park display bright red Grinnell mudstone and stark white sandstone in vivid contrast.

The Siyeh Limestone

Pale gray cliffs of Siyeh limestone tower above the red Grinnell mudstones to dominate the high country in most of the central part of Glacier Park. The formation is about 3,500 feet thick and, more than any other, is the rock that park visitors see.

Many exposures of Siyeh limestone contain fossil algal structures called "stromatolites" that look

Left: Grinnell Glacier from helicopter. — Mel Ruder
Top: Stromatolite, ancient algal structures, showing beside the road at Logan Pass. This photo shows an area about 15 feet across. — Dave Alt
Above: Ripple marks formed in an ancient sea bed show in this boulder at 6,800 feet atop Boulder Pass. — Pete and Alice Bengeyfield.
Opposite Page: Mount Wilbur showing the Purcell sill as the distinct band of black rock with white above and below near the peaks. — Gordon Sullivan

almost as though they might be fossil cabbages. Exactly similar structures grow today in a few places, so we know that stromatolites are the remains of extremely primitive blue-green algae. We are all familiar with blue-green algae as the plant that forms scummy growths in puddles, covers the north side of trees and rocks, and infests fish tanks. Stromatolites range from a few inches to several feet in diameter, and they commonly form reefs that completely fill entire layers of rock. Some of the ledges of Siyeh limestone around Logan Pass and along the trail to Hidden Lake contain excellent stromatolites. Similar fossils exist locally, and less abundantly, in the Altyn limestone and the red mudstones. We should all view those fossils with respect and admiration as early pioneers who led the way for other forms of life. We would not be here now had they not been here then.

Primitive though they are, blue-green algae are green plants that do absorb atmospheric carbon dioxide, produce organic matter, and release oxygen to the atmosphere. Stromatolites in the Siyeh limestone are probably the remains of plants that began the long process of removing most of the carbon dioxide from the earth's early atmosphere, and releasing oxygen to create the kind of air animals can breathe.

Of course, an atom of carbon buried in sedimentary rocks must balance every molecule of oxygen in the atmosphere to account for the original carbon dioxide. The Siyeh limestone is dark in fresh exposures because it contains organic matter, so much in some places that freshly broken rock smells putrid. That billion-year-old odor of decay is one of the reasons that the air we breathe contains oxygen.

The Purcell Diabase Sill

The upper part of the Siyeh formation contains a conspicuous layer about 100 feet thick of black igneous rock called "diabase" sandwiched between layers of limestone. Molten magma squirted between sedimentary layers to form the layer of igneous rock. Geologists call an igneous intrusion formed that way a "sill." Precambrian sedimentary rocks throughout the northern Rocky Mountains contain hundreds of thick sills. This particularly conspicuous and well know example in Glacier Park is called the "Purcell sill."

Heat from the magma drove the dark organic stain out of the Siyeh limestone above and below the sill, bleaching it white. So the sill appears as a nearly horizontal black band bordered in white above and below, a conspicuous striped ribbon on many of the

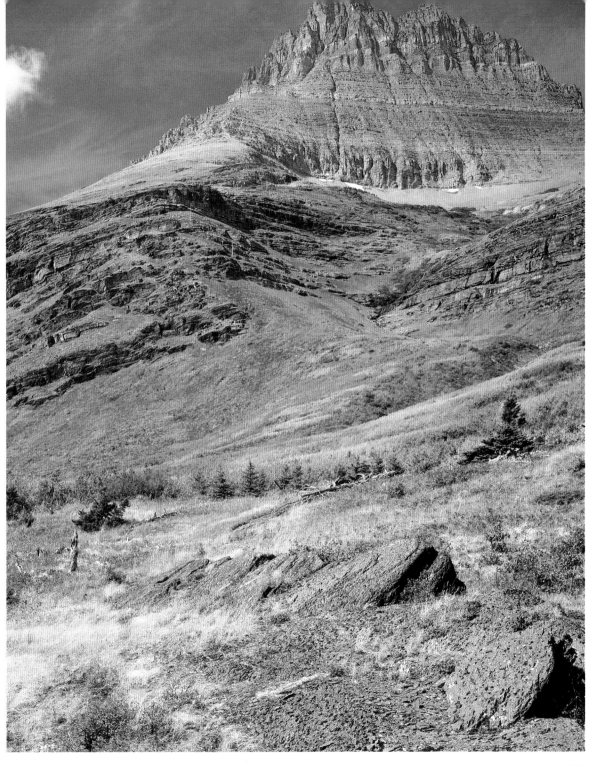

cliffs high in the park. Several roadcuts at the top of Logan Pass expose the Purcell sill, and the Logan Pass end of the trail to Granite Park passes several outstanding exposures of the sill, and of the bleached limestone near its borders.

At Granite Park, the Purcell sill turns into a lava flow of the kind that geologists call "pillow basalt." The magma evidently erupted into the water in which the Siyeh limestone was accumulating, and formed a pile of cylindrical masses that look a bit like oversized pillows where we see them exposed in an outcrop. Lavas that erupt under water generally do that.

Age dates obtained by analyzing the radioactive elements in diabase from the Purcell sill show that it is slightly more than one billion years old. That must also be the age of the upper part of the Siyeh limestone, because the sill erupted a lava flow into the formation while it was still soft and muddy. Therefore, all the rocks below the Siyeh limestone must be more than one billion years old, perhaps much more. The rocks above are at least a bit less than one billion years old. We have no better clue to the age of the rocks in the park than the exposures at Granite Park.

Despite the name, there is no granite at Granite Park, or anywhere else in or even near Glacier Park. Even though the diabase of the Purcell sill vaguely resembles granite in that both are speckled igneous rocks, the two rocks differ in most important respects. Most obviously, granite is very pale gray, diabase very dark gray, almost black in many places. Pieces of diabase from the Purcell sill are common nearly everywhere in the park. Watch the stream beds for pebbles of dark gray rock speckled with light crystals of feldspar about the size of rice grains.

The Shepard and Kintla Formations

The trail from the visitor center at Logan Pass to Hidden Lake is one of the best places to see the Shepard formation, about 1,000 feet of mostly red and tan mudstone. Nearly every outcrop along the higher part of that route is a natural museum of beautiful ripple marks and mudcracks, still exquisitely preserved almost a billion years after they formed. The upper part of the formation blends into about 1,000 feet of red mudstones that geologists call the Kintla formation. Most people look at the Kintla mudstones from a distance, becuase there is no place to see them at close range without a strenuous climb. Look at the red caps on many of the high mountains near the middle of the park.

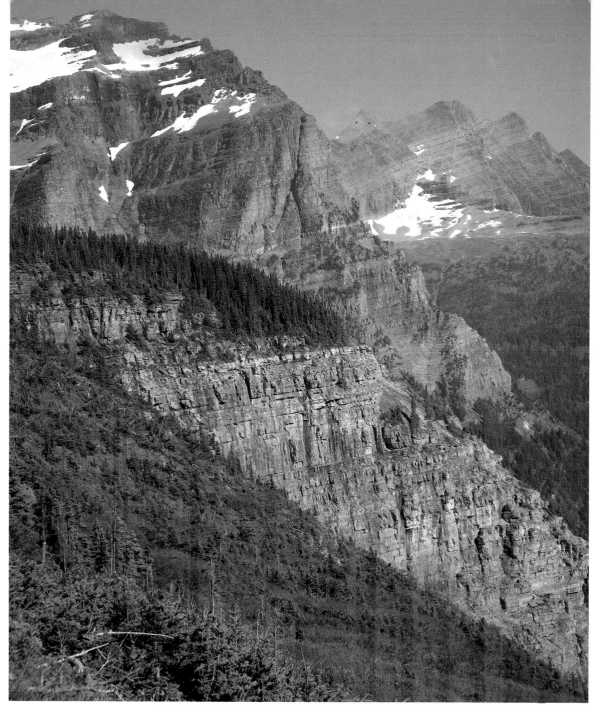

Above: Jagged edges of valleys formed by glaciers in the Brown's Pass area in northern Glacier Park. This view is to the west from the pass toward Kintla Lake.

— Gordon Sullivan

Opposite Page: Granite Park area. — Gordon Sullivan

The Shepard and Kintla formations are the youngest Precambrian rocks in the park. Even they contain no hint of the abundant animal life that would appear on earth a few hundred million years after they formed. In fact, the perfect preservation of very fine sedimentary details such as ripple marks and mudcracks in these rocks strongly suggests that animals had not yet appeared. In more recent times, digging and crawling animals have generally destroyed such structures long before the original soft sediments could harden into rock.

The Lewis Overthrust

So far as anyone knows, the rocks we see in Glacier Park lay undisturbed until the Rocky Mountains formed sometime around 65 million years ago, give or take 10 million. All sorts of complex things happened as the Rocky Mountains formed, and the details need not concern us here because they do not greatly affect what we see in the park. One event that we do see clearly expressed in the landscape of Glacier Park was movement on the Lewis overthrust fault.

The large slab of Precambrian sedimentary rock that we see in the park slid eastward down a gently sloping surface that geologists call the "Lewis overthrust fault." No one knows exactly where the slab of Precambrian sedimentary rock came from, or exactly how far it moved. It must have come at least 35 miles, perhaps as far as 50 miles, conceivably farther. Neither does anyone know how long that movement lasted, but it was certainly not sudden, and probably continued for several million years at an imperceptibly slow pace. The fault appears in the landscape of the eastern part of the park.

At the Lewis overthrust fault, steep hills and cliffs of hard Precambrian rock rise abruptly above a

Top: Mount Crandell above Waterton, Alberta shows large folds in billion-year-old sedimentary rocks near the leading edge of the Lewis overthrust slab. — Dave Alt
Bottom: Chief Mountain, a landmark on the eastern fringe of the park, is also a perfect expression of overthrust geology. Ancient precambrian rock sits atop (overthrust upon) much younger rock. The Lewis fault is at the break in slope at the base of the mountain. — D. W. Hyndman

softly rolling landscape eroded on much softer rocks beneath. The line of the fault exactly traces the eastern front of the mountains, where the rugged landscape of the Rocky Mountains meets the open expanse of the northern high plains. People driving beside St. Mary Lake cross the fault at the narrows near Rising Sun Campground, at a cliff of Altyn limestone.

Precambrian rocks above the Lewis overthrust fault lie on top of Cretaceous brown sandstones and black mudstones only about 100 million years old, the same rocks that lie beneath the high plains east of the park. The Cretaceous rocks below the Lewis overthrust fault accumulated in shallow sea water at the western margin of an island sea that then flooded much of central North America. Animal fossils do exist in the Cretaceous rocks, but they are hard to find because the Cretaceous rocks weather easily, and form very few good exposures.

The Lewis overthrust fault reverses the normal state of affairs in which the youngest rocks lie at the top of the stack, the oldest at the bottom. Glacier Park was one of the first places geologists found overthrust faults of this kind back in the 1890s, and it remains among the best places to see an overthrust fault. The best way to obtain a grand view of the Lewis overthrust fault is to look north from the top of Marias Pass on Highway 2 at the mountains in the southern edge of the park. You can see the tan Altyn limestone just above the fault as a straight band of tan rock that slopes like a railway grade descending gently down to the west.

We see the Lewis overthrust fault most perfectly expressed in Chief Mountain, a block of Precambrian sedimentary rock isolated by erosion from the rest of the overthrust slab. On all sides of Chief Mountain, the hard Precambrian sedimentary rocks rise in steep cliffs above the much softer Cretaceous sedimentary rocks that surround the mountain and continue beneath it.

The North Fork Valley

We see another aspect of the Lewis overthrust fault in the North Fork Valley, which trends along the western margin of the park. It is about ten miles wide, much too broad to be an ordinary river valley. The width of that valley, and its remarkably straight north-to-south course, suggest that it must reflect bedrock structure. It seems reasonably clear that the North Fork Valley is a gap in the overthrust slab.

The Whitefish Range, west of the North Fork Valley, contains Precambrian sedimentary formations like those in Glacier Park. In Canada, only a few miles from Glacier Park, Cretaceous formations similar to those exposed in the high plains come to the surface in the floor of the North Fork Valley. We would surely see the same formations in the western part of Glacier Park if the younger glacial sediments did not so completely cover the older rocks there.

The easiest way to explain the presence of Cretaceous rocks in the North Fork Valley is to assume that the overthrust slab broke into two pieces. The fragment destined to become Glacier Park moved ten miles farther east than the one that became the Whitefish Range. So the North Fork Valley is a window between the two parts of the overthrust slab. It looks down into the relatively young Cretaceous formations beneath the ancient sedimentary rocks that we see in the mountains on either side. Compare the slab of Precambrian rock that slid east on the Lewis overthrust fault to a slab of snow sliding down a roof, and then imagine the slab of snow separating into two large pieces exposing the roof between them.

Eroding the Modern Landscape

Movement on the Lewis overthrust fault created the major elements of the landscape; the blocks of mountains you might see from the moon, not the individual hills and valleys. Those are the legacy of at least 50 million years of patient erosional sculpture that still continues.

During most of the last 50 million or more years, the region had a desert climate, and erosion created landscapes much like those we see in the southwest desert today. Then, during the last two to three million years, a series of great ice ages brought enormous glaciers that carved most of the details of the modern landscape.

The Desert Years

During most of the past 50 million years, the entire region has had an extremely dry climate, perhaps similar to that of the modern southwest deserts. By the end of that time, streams had dissected the mountains of Glacier Park into a maze of deep and closely spaced canyons, and deposited the debris of their erosion in a blanket of gravel spread far to the east. Although little, if anything, of the old desert landscape survives in the mountains, we can still see large remnants of the old high plains surface east of the mountains.

Erosion in dry regions tends to produce large expanses of smoothly graded plains underlain by layers of gravel laid down during occasional flash floods. Such plains did exist east of Glacier Park, east all the way to the Dakotas. The climate became wetter when the ice ages began, sometime between two and three million years ago, and modern streams have since carved their valleys into the old desert plains surface. Now, we see remnants of that old surface in the high uplands between streams. Look for their flat skyline profiles in the landscapes east of the mountain front.

The Ice Ages

Sometime between two and three million years ago the earth's climate changed, and great ice ages have come and gone ever since. No one knows what causes the great ice ages, or what ends them. Neither does anyone know how many ice ages there were, when they happened, or how long they lasted. Nor do we know when the next ice age will start, or what may herald its coming.

Those interesting and important questions need not concern us here. The glaciers that covered most of Glacier Park during the last ice age nearly obliterated the record of their predecessors, leaving a landscape that could as well have been created during a single ice age as during several. Almost everything we see in the modern landscape emerged in essentially its present form as the glaciers of the last ice age melted about 10,000 years ago.

During the height of the last ice age, glaciers as much as several thousand feet thick filled all the valleys in the park. Adjacent glaciers coalesced in many places to spread a nearly continuous ice cap over much of the high country. Many of the mountain glaciers in the western part of the park flowed into the North Fork Valley, ponding there to make a slowly moving sheet of ice ten miles across.

East of the park, glaciers pouring out of the mountains ponded on the high plains to make a broad expanse of nearly stagnant ice, a "piedmont glacier" along the mountain front. Somewhere between Glacier Park and Browning, that piedmont glacier met and coalesced with the continental glacier spreading southwestward from central Canada. The seam is not obvious in the landscape, but we can determine just where the two glaciers joined by finding the line where glacially transported rocks from the Rocky Mountains meet the entirely different rocks carried in from northern Manitoba.

15

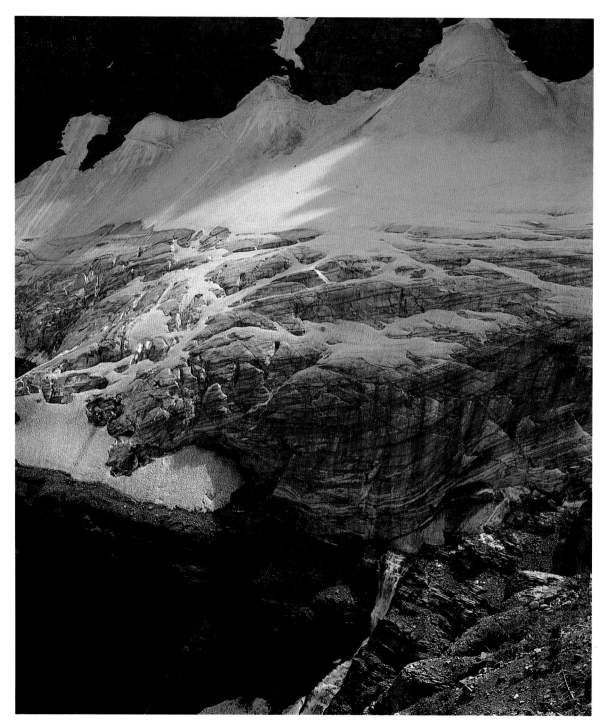

Glaciers

If more snow falls every winter than can melt the next summer, leftover snow accumulates from year to year and slowly turns into solid ice. As the ice reaches a depth of about 150 feet, it begins to flow plastically, as though it were extremely stiff modelling clay. When that happens, the patch of ice becomes a glacier. Some glaciers are hardly more than oversized snow patches, but those that carved the landscape of Glacier Park were real ice age monsters, rivers of ice miles long and as much as several thousand feet deep in some places.

So far as anyone knows, glaciers that form on mountains never create new valleys. Instead, they invariably pour ponderously down stream valleys that already existed, changing them into glaciated stream valleys. Glaciers erode their valleys in some places, deposit the eroded sediments in others. The final result, after the ice melts, is a distinctive landscape that tells of glaciation in nearly every detail.

As a glacier moves down its valley, it descends into warmer climates, eventually reaching a level where the ice melts as fast as it advances. That balance stabilizes the front of the ice until the climate changes. An increase in the snowfall at high elevation will push the snout of the glacier to lower elevations, where the climate is warm enough to match the increased ice flow. Conversely, decreased snowfall at high elevations will reduce ice flow, causing the snout of the glacier to melt back to a higher, and cooler, elevation. As we might expect, glaciers respond to a warming climate by melting back to higher elevations, to a cooling climate by advancing to lower elevations.

The Depth of the Ice

Glaciers carry enormous quantities of mud, sand and gravel embedded in the ice, especially in the lower part of the glacier. All that sediment makes the sole of the glacier rasp across bedrock surfaces as though it were a giant sheet of coarse sandpaper. After the glacier melts, the rasped bedrock surfaces are left smoothed, and covered with sets of parallel grooves called striations. Look almost anywhere in the park for such crudely sandpapered bedrock surfaces. The striations record the exact direction of ice movement. On a larger scale, the smoothed bedrock surfaces preserve a record of where the ice flowed, and where other processes of erosion shaped the bedrock. That record still survives in some areas of Glacier Park 10,000 years after the great glaciers melted.

Look high up the cliffs almost anywhere in the park to see that their lower parts are relatively smooth, their highest parts extremely rough. The smooth lower parts and rougher upper part meet along a sharp line that slopes gently down the valley. That line marks the ice level on the cliff during the height of the last ice age. Sediment embedded in the glacier rasped the lower part of the cliff smooth, while freezing and thawing pried blocks out of the rock above the ice, leaving that part of the cliff ragged. The old ice level is especially easy to see on the cliffs high above Logan Pass and Two Medicine Lake.

In areas where the old ice level is still well preserved, it is possible to trace it with the eye from one mountain side to another to reconstruct mentally the glaciers that existed during the last ice age. By doing that, we can see that ice completely filled many valleys and spilled over the divides between them to coalesce with a glacier in the next valley. Many large areas of the park must have lain beneath an almost continuous ice cap. In much of Glacier Park only the higher peaks rose above the expanse of ice.

Opposite Page, Left: Sexton Glacier from the Siyeh Pass trail showing the almost plastic consistency of glacial ice as opposed to snowpack. — Bruce Selyem
Opposite Page, Right: The sole of a glacier is like sandpaper, literally scouring rock layers beneath it. This is "striated" Shepard mudstone near Hidden Lake, showing an area about 3 feet across. — Dave Alt
This Page: Excellent example of a cirque at the base of Pollock Mountain. — Jeff Gnass

The Giant Quarrying Machine

Glaciers erode bedrock mostly by freezing fast to blocks of rock already broken along ancient fractures, and then pulling them loose, a process called "plucking." Glacially plucked bedrock surfaces have a ragged look, as though they had been crudely quarried. Look at almost any of the high cliffs in the park to see examples of glacially plucked surfaces.

The heads of glaciers pluck chunks of bedrock loose more efficiently than any other part. As it moves downslope, the ice draws away from the bedrock behind it, pulling blocks of bedrock loose and opening a gap between rock and ice. Anyone who walks to the head of a glacier must cross that gap to get back onto bedrock, and in many cases that requires quite a jump. Snow and meltwater fill that gap with new ice that freezes fast to the bedrock. Meanwhile, the glacier continues to move down its valley and so repeats the process, pulling more chunks of rock loose, and opening again the gap between ice and bedrock. Now that the ice has melted, we can see how deeply the heads of the ice age glaciers quarried the mountain tops.

Every glacial valley heads in a large hollow called a "cirque," perhaps the most characteristic element of glaciated mountain landscapes. There are hundreds of cirques in Glacier Park. Nearly every peak drops away into cirques on at least one side, most on several sides. In many places, adjacent cirques blend into each other, making it hard to see them individually. In other places, cirques stand alone, looking as though a giant had gouged the mountain with an oversized ice cream scoop. Sparkling little lakes nestle in the floors of many cirques, reflecting the cliffs of the headwall rising to the peak above. Hidden Lake, Avalanche Lake, and Iceberg Lake are all good examples of cirque lakes familiar to many park visitors.

Where several glaciers flowed down a mountain, gouging cirques into the summit from several directions, we now see the jagged remnant of the original peak. It forms a ragged pinnacle that drops away in steep cliffs into the deep cirques below. We call those rocky spires "horn" peaks, an alpine term familiar in the names of such famous mountains as the Matterhorn. Most of the high peaks in Glacier Park are horns.

Gouged Valleys

Every summer, people expose thousands of dollars of film recording views of distant peaks reflected in the waters of Lake McDonald or St. Mary Lake. Those really are remarkable scenes, and they could

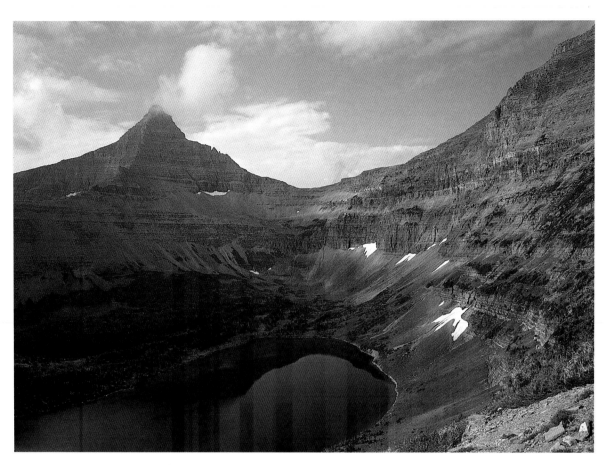

Above: Oldman Lake west of the Two Medicine area is a tarn or lake formed in a cirque. Behind it stands Flinsch Peak, a horn peak. — Gordon Sullivan

Opposite Page: The famed Garden Wall is an "arete" to geologists. — Jeff Gnass

not exist if the great ice age glaciers had not gouged the valleys straight so we could look along them at the mountains in the distance.

Glaciers are less flexible than rivers, and cannot flow so easily around bends in the valleys. So, they remove the bends from the original river valley as though they were bulldozers going down a narrow mountain trail. Of course, that also leaves the valley considerably wider than it was before glaciation. And it changes the cross-sectional profile.

Large glaciers tend to gouge their valleys into deeply rounded troughs almost semi-circular in cross-section. We see that best in the higher parts of glaciated valleys where very little sediment fills the floor. The bedrock floors of those high parts of the

glaciated valley typically contain small lakes or ponds called "tarns." You can tell that tarns fill a bedrock basin by going to the outlet stream and watching it spill over solid rock.

Glaciers gnaw the ridges separating adjacent valleys into thin rock walls with ragged crests generally called "aretes," a term imported from the Swiss Alps where the glaciated landscapes resemble those in Glacier Park. The Garden Wall is a good example of an arete familiar to many park visitors. It is so thin near its crest that in one place there is a hole in it. In the Many Glacier area, people enjoy watching the sun shine for a moment through that window as it sets behind the Garden Wall. Before glaciation, that thin wall of rock was the crest of a broad ridge.

Where active glaciers meet, their surfaces join at the same level. Now that the ice has melted and exposed the floors of those glaciated valleys, we can see that small glaciers do not carve as deeply as do large glaciers. Tributary valleys stand well above the main valley, and their streams join the main stream over waterfalls or cascades. Most park visitors see Birdwoman Falls as they drive along the valley of McDonald Creek.

Glacial Moraines

Melting glacial ice dumps a deposit of indiscriminately mixed mud, sand, gravel, and boulders. That material, which looks in a roadcut like something a bulldozer might have scraped together, is called "till." It is easy to recognize even where there is no roadcut because glaciers leave boulders littering the surfaces of most deposits. Geologists call any deposit of till a "moraine."

There are several kinds of moraines that differ in origin according to the part of the glacier that deposited them, and also differ in appearance. Let's start with the most distinctive kind.

Glaciers deposit a ridge of till around their lower margins where a balance between the rates of ice advance and melting puts an end to the glacial conveyor belt. The result is a "terminal moraine" that faithfully records the outline of the lower part of the

Opposite Page: Snow and sun emphasize the "plucked cliffs" effect of Garden Wall. — Gordon Sullivan
Above: Red Rock Lake is retained by a moraine, as are most of the glacial lakes in the park. — Gordon Sullivan

glacier that built it. We don't see very many good examples of terminal moraines within Glacier Park, because so many of the valley glaciers emptied into either the big piedmont ice sheet along the eastern margin of the park, or the huge glacier that filled the North Fork Valley. However, there are a few small moraines at high elevations that appear to have formed since the last ice age ended.

Glaciers also deposit till along their margins to build "lateral moraines," which make high benches along the valley walls. Lateral moraines are especially prominent on south-facing valley walls at low elevations because more ice melts in those places, and therefore deposits more sediment. Large lateral moraines exist along the lower parts of most of the valleys in the park, and in some places they become very prominent indeed. The ridges on both sides of Lake McDonald, for example, are large lateral

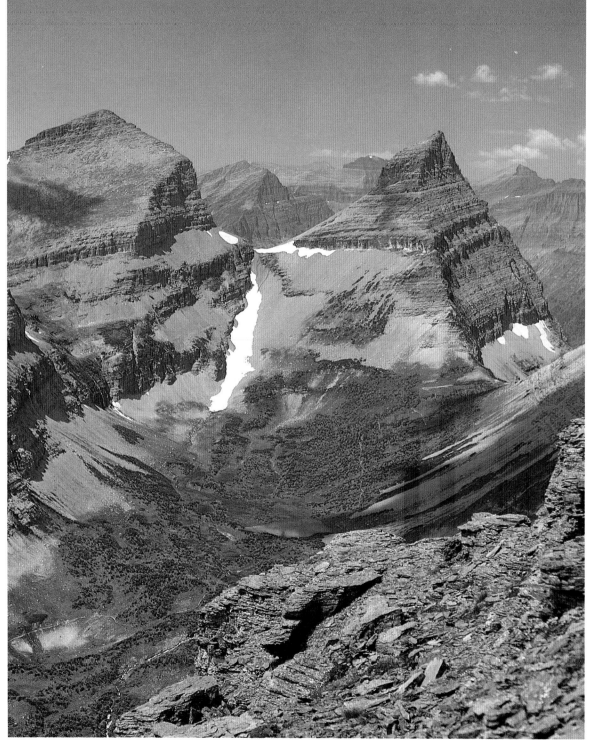

moraines, perhaps the most spectacular in the park. And the densely wooded hills along the south side of St. Mary Lake are other large lateral moraines.

Finally, melting glaciers plaster much of the ground beneath them with till to create a rather characterless deposit called a "ground moraine." Most of the large valleys in the park have ground moraine here and there in their floors, but we rarely notice them except as expanses of gently undulating valley floor full of small ponds and marshes. Glacial till is generally fairly impermeable to water, and ground moraine is especially so because it was compacted beneath the weight of the glacier.

Glacial Outwash

We think of ice ages as cold times, and the climate probably was significantly colder than what we know today, also much wetter. However, there is no reason to doubt that ice age summers were warm, quite possibly as warm as the summers we know. The summer days were long then too, and many must have been sunny. We are, after all, descended from people who camped out during the last ice age, and our ancestors seem to have managed quite well.

We know, because we can see the results, that vast quantities of ice melted off the lower parts of the ice age glaciers every summer, shedding torrents of muddy water into the streams. The swollen and muddy streams dropped part of their sediment load to form deposits that geologists call "outwash." We can look at the streams that drain from glaciers in Alaska and Canada today, and imagine what ours must have been like then: many small and constantly shifting channels picking their way through a maze of islands. But the muddiest season came as the glaciers melted at the end of the ice age.

Everything we see suggests that the last ice age ended abruptly. At the height of the last ice age, about eleven or twelve thousand years ago, so much

Left: A classic horn peak seen from below Pyramid Peak, Stoney Indian Pass at the right base of the horn. — Rick Gractz

Opposite Page Left: Glacial outwash, Grinnell Glacier. — Bert Gildart

Opposite Page, Right: Less than a mile from the murky runoff from Iceberg Lake, the stream is a beautiful mountain brook. — Gordon Sullivan

water was tied up in the great glaciers that sea level stood some 300 feet lower than it now does. Then the climate changed, and within 2,500 years sea level had risen to its present stand, which means that the land ice had melted back to about what we see today. Even though we don't know how or why the climate changed, we can easily imagine what Glacier Park was like during those 2,500 years.

The place was, quite simply, a mess.

Rapidly melting glaciers shed torrents of incredibly muddy water, and leave behind them dreary expanses of watery mud and gravel. In Glacier Park, all that debris still lies just as the melting glaciers left it about 10,000 years ago. Nothing has changed except that trees have grown since then, and they make things look nicer. Consider Lake McDonald and St. Mary Lake, both relics of the last years of the last ice age.

Meanwhile, the tediously slow processes of weather are beginning to break the bare rock down into soil, and thus to soften the harsh outlines of the glaciated mountains. However, that is an extremely slow process, and one cannot help wondering how far it may progress before another ice age intervenes. To see how slowly weathering proceeds, look at the glacially striated bedrock surfaces almost anywhere in the park, and remember that they have probably been ice free and exposed to the elements for approximately 10,000 years. It is impossible to ponder the freshness of those surfaces without reflecting that soil is not a renewable resource within any humanly meaningful time span, and that soil erosion really does impose an irreparable loss.

Finally, the modern glaciers: Compared to their predecessors of the last ice age, they are nothing. And they have diminished greatly in both size and number since they were first mapped just after the turn of the century. Such small, perhaps minuscule is the better word, glaciers could not by any stretch of the imagination carve the magnificent landscape we see in Glacier Park. Furthermore, the little glaciers we see in the park today appear to be new glaciers that formed sometime after the last ice age, not the shrunken remnants of the ice age giants. The modern glaciers have carved small cirques around the edges of some of the big cirques left from the last ice age, and they have made a few moraines high in the mountains. Otherwise, they have contributed very little to the landscape of Glacier Park.

But who knows? Someday those little glaciers we see in the highest and shadiest valleys of Glacier Park may grow into the next generation of giants when the next ice age begins.

Lake McDonald formed as the glaciers melted. Evidently, a large mass of ice was left behind as the glacier rapidly melted back, and muddy meltwater washed sediment in around it, perhaps partially burying it. When that marooned expanse of ice finally melted some hundreds or perhaps thousands of years later, it left the basin that the lake now fills. St. Mary Lake formed at the same time, although in a different way. Glacial meltwater washing into the valley from tributary canyons on both sides deposited large fans of gravel that now impound the lake. The park entrance and visitor center at the lower end of St. Mary Lake stand on that deposit of gravel. Similar situations exist in the lower parts of most of the large valleys in the park.

Now that the great ice age glaciers are gone, at least for the time being, other processes of erosion are slowly changing the mountains of Glacier Park. Nevertheless, most of what we see is still left from the last ice age, not the product of modern processes of erosion.

Now streams of water flow along the floors of valleys that were filled to the brim with ice a little more than 10,000 years ago. The water is slowly shaping the floors of those valleys into the forms that streams create, but they have not made much progress. The waterfalls and cascades are all remnants of glacial erosion, and will all disappear as the streams continue their own work.

The big lakes trap most of the sediment that the modern streams carry and every particle of mud or grain of sand brings the lake closer to its end. Before too many thousands of years have passed, all the lakes will have filled with sediment, and become level plains. In the geologic sense of time, all lakes are temporary, and doomed to quick disappearance.

After the Ice Age

Above Left: Trenches in the foreground are the exposed edges of rock layers tilted to the earth. Imagine looking at the edge of a giant sloppy stack of pancakes. This exposure is near Grinnell Glacier. — Bert Gildart
Opposite Page: The story of Glacier's past is found not only in its magnificent landscape but also in the rocks themselves.
(A) Water seeping between rock layers or "bedding surfaces" in Siyeh Limestone near Logan Pass. — Dave Alt
(B) Massive yet rather elegant rock folding at Sperry Glacier. — Mel Ruder
(C) Ripple marks in sandstone a billion years in age. — Dave Alt
(D) Glacial till. The unconsolidated, indiscriminate mix of rocks, sand, gravel and mud is distinctly glacial. — Dave Alt

A

B

C

D

25

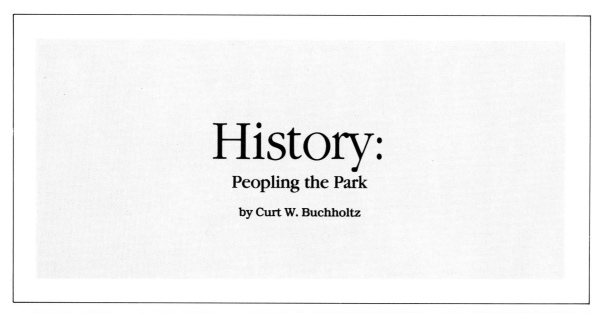

History:
Peopling the Park

by Curt W. Buchholtz

Glacier's rocky peaks, deep-blue lakes and dense forests have long put out a call to people. Primitive pathways must have lured Native American hunters, and we know its cliffs and echoes made enough magic to stimulate legends. The fur trade brought a handful of trappers and traders cautiously venturing through. Mountain passes caught the eyes of railroad engineers and likely looking rocks kept prospectors prowling. Vacant land drew pioneers. Scenic land brought tourists. The abuse of land made conservationists decide to protect this region, and simple aesthetics made others wish to preserve it for future generations. Solitude and natural beauty attracted people looking for rest and recreation.

The wilderness itself reminds us of the past, the way things used to look. It offers a stark contrast to everyday scenes crowded with cars and concrete. Its wilderness makes us wonder about all those earlier travelers who heard the mountains' call. Even an outline of their visits may help us appreciate what little wild country remains, still preserved for our pleasure.

Tribes and Trails

Exactly who first traveled the trails of today's Glacier Park remains a mystery. Someday archeologists may find an ancient campsite, a cache of tools, or some other clues to provide us with a clearer prehistoric picture. Meanwhile, we can only speculate about ancient hunters who haunted these mountains. Chances are good that prehistoric hunters roamed through this region thousands of years ago, but evidence of their activity is scant. A few circles of rocks marking old tepee rings still may be spotted along the eastern foothills. An old buffalo skull once was found atop Chief Mountain. But stones and bones merely hint at Indian pursuits of religious beliefs. For the most part, Glacier's prehistory remains a mystery.

Left: Blackfeet Indians at Cracker Lake. — Courtesy, Glacier Park
Opposite Page: Cosley Lake. — Gordon Sullivan

Our first documented glimpse of the region was provided by Hudson Bay Company agent Peter Fidler. He was traveling with a Piegan band of Blackfeet Indians, southwestward across the Canadian prairies in 1792. A map Fidler later produced displayed a rough sketch of the Rockies and the name of "Kings Mountain" attached to one of those peaks. Later changed to "Chief Mountain," that prominent landmark of the front range became the first of Glacier's features to gain recognition. What Peter Fidler also discovered, as did a few other traders who probed this area, was the fact that powerful bands of Blackfeet (Blackfoot is also acceptable) Indians dominated the entire upper Missouri River region and the headwaters of the Saskatchewan River as well.

At that time the Blackfeet Confederation consisted of the Siksika (or Northern Blackfeet), the Kainah (or Bloods), and the Piegan (or Pikuni). Allied with them were the Gros Ventre (or Big Belly). These warlike bands had extended their power throughout the plains during the 1700s, just after they obtained horses and guns. Their reputation as fearsome warriors spread quickly. Their dominion included vast herds of bison, now theirs to hunt. With plentiful food, and hides for clothing, shelter and equipment the Blackfeet clearly were masters of Montana's northern plains by the 1790s. For them, Glacier's Rockies acted as a massive western boundary. And upon occasion, small raiding parties of aggressive Blackfeet ventured across the mountains to prey upon tribes of the western slope. Glacier's high passes served those war parties well. Very rarely did the Blackfeet bother to hunt mountain animals, however, since their horses and lifestyle were geared to the prairie.

More accustomed to the mountains were several Indian tribes far less powerful than the Blackfeet. The Kutenai, the Kalispel (or Pend d'Oreille) and the Flathead tribes ranged throughout the forested valleys of western Montana. Until the Blackfeet forced them off the plains, these tribes also had lived and hunted on the prairie. In making the mountains their home, deer and elk, fish and fowl, berries and camas roots became their staples — all substitutes for the favored buffalo. Once or twice a year, hunting parties from these western tribes bravely ventured east across the mountains, entering the plains to hunt buffalo at the risk of a Blackfeet attack. One rare tale of such a clash placed the event near Glacier's Cut Bank Creek. There Siyeh (Mad Wolf) and his band of Blackfeet warriors fought some Kutenai

Above Left: James Willard Schultz and friends. Schultz lived among the Blackfeet as a young man before the tribe was reservation bound. — Courtesy, Glacier Park
Above Right: Two Guns White Calf, one of the Indians
who modeled for the buffalo nickel. — Courtesy, Glacier Park
Opposite Page: Blackfeet at Trick Falls, about 1917. — Courtesy, Montana Historical Society

who were attempting to return westward across Cut Bank Pass. There the Blackfeet, according to the tale, slaughtered and scalped all the Kutenai except for one old woman.

Violence and hostility kept the western tribes confined to the mountains. But their lifestyles adjusted quickly. The Kutenai, in particular, developed a reputation for being skilled hunters of mountain sheep. Observers marveled at their ability to run up steep slopes and early explorers noted that their leg muscles developed an abnormal size from climbing across ridges.

Another minor band of Indians also frequented the region. Called the Mountain Assiniboine (or Stonies), this group subsisted along the eastern foothills. Forced by the Blackfeet to accept less desirable hunting grounds, the Stonies gained their name from their method of cooking food with heated rocks. The Stonies were few in number and always fearful of their more aggressive neighbors. Deer and elk served as their food supply, with lesser animals like porcupine adding to their diet when hunting was bad, as did chewing the bark of trees if starvation was imminent.

Years of hunting and warfare sparked numerous legends and tales. Writers like George Bird Grinnell of the 1880s and James Willard Schultz of the 1920s recorded many Indian stories, some associated with Glacier's mountains. Grinnell's stories of Napi (or Old Man) and the Blackfeet Genesis are particularly poignant. As a result of Grinnell and Schultz' writings, a pantheon of Indian chiefs and

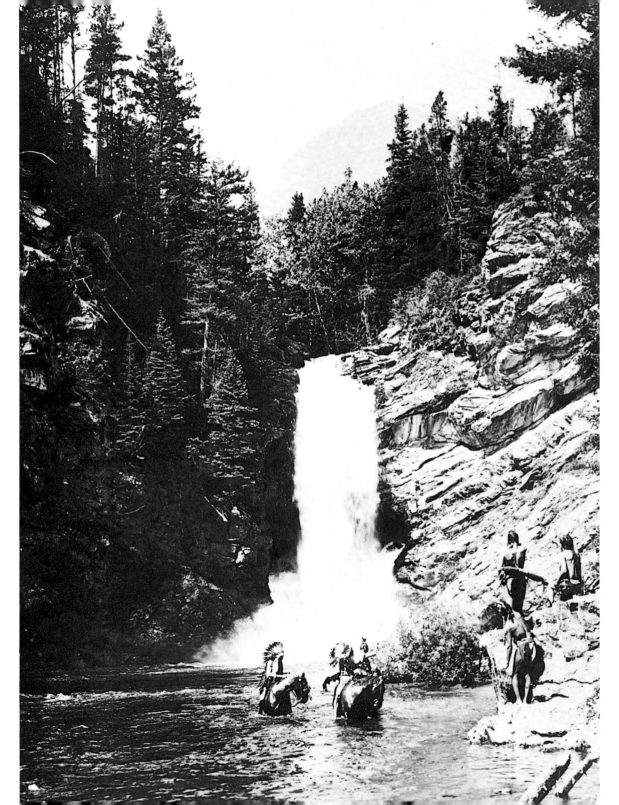

heroes' names became attached to Glacier's landscape. Dotting the map are Red Eagle, Curly Bear, Heavy Runner and Mad Wolf, all recalling famous Indian leaders. Medicine Grizzly, Beaver Medicine and Windmaker evoke the stuff of legends. A few Indian names predated Grinnell and Schultz, with Two Medicine Valley obtaining its name from two ceremonial lodges which once graced that region. Saint Mary Lakes were called The Lakes Inside before white man arrived. Many other Indian names help memorialize their early presence in this area.

Through much of the 19th century Blackfeet power kept visitors or invaders away from this territory. Not until constant war, recurrent smallpox epidemics and whiskey reduced their numbers and will to fight did the Blackfeet weaken their grip upon this land. Gradually trappers and trading posts became more common. Disappearing buffalo herds spelled the end of the prosperity of food and materials, and starvation was common among the Blackfeet by the 1880s. At the same time, prospectors were demanding that the Blackfeet relinquish their mountain land. In 1895, the Blackfeet sold the "Ceded Strip" (Glacier's eastern side) for $1.5 million. Decades earlier, western slope tribes relinquished any claims to these mountains. Still, today's Blackfeet Reservation, adjacent to Glacier's eastern boundary, reminds us of earlier Native American stewardship over the entire region.

Trappers and Travelers

Indian hostility kept most mountain men away from Glacier. Only a handful of trappers or traders left any account of their journeys across these mountains. In 1810, for one rare example, trapper Finian MacDonald and 150 Indian allies crossed through Marias Pass headed toward the plains. Almost immediately they encountered 170 "Peeagans." The ensuing battle left seven Blackfeet dead and taught men like MacDonald to choose safer routes far to the north or south. Other fur traders simply skirted the region. And only sketchy evidence links the search for beaver pelts with Glacier's waterways. Both Lake McDonald and tiny Rubideau Creek may derive their names from such adventurers.

Missionaries and map makers also traveled through quickly. Exactly which "Black Robe" paused to christen Saint Mary Lake remains a question,

29

but maps soon would display that appellation. In the early 1850s "official" explorers began arriving. Engineer A. W. Tinkham, associated with the Isaac I. Stevens' survey, traveled across Glacier in 1853 as he searched for potential railroad routes. He crossed Cut Bank Pass and noted that any railroad built there would require a huge tunnel. The following years Stevens dispatched John Doty, who more carefully surveyed all of Glacier's eastern slope. But Doty concluded that none of the mountain passes he observed were suitable for railroads, leaving Marias Pass to be "rediscovered" in 1889 by another engineer, John F. Stevens.

Other government surveyors arrived by 1860, this time marking the 49th parallel as the international boundary. With them came artist James Madison Alden, who produced the first scenic watercolors of Glacier's northern mountains. By the 1860s and 1870s a few prospectors wandered along the western slope. In one sketchy (albeit surprising) report, a 30-ounce nugget of gold supposedly was found at Quartz Lake. Those decades also introduced a few itinerate whiskey traders, plying their products among the Indians along the eastern slope. One such "whiskey fort" established by John Kennedy is remembered only by the name of today's Kennedy Creek.

Additional government surveys in 1874 brought Lt. John Van Orsdale, dispatched to observe this area from Fort Shaw. After visiting Lake McDonald (which he called Lake Terry after his commanding officer), traveling up Nyack Creek, and crossing Cut Bank Pass, Van Orsdale was sufficiently impressed by the country to write a letter suggesting that the region be made a national park. With Yellowstone Park founded only two years earlier, Van Orsdale believed he had spotted another national treasure. But more than two decades would pass before others found merit in his suggestion.

The 1880s ushered in the man who would insure that the national park idea would succeed. As an authority on Indians and as editor of *Forest and Stream* magazine, George Bird Grinnell was influential as well as politically knowledgeable. He originally came to the region to publicize the starving and destitute condition of the Blackfeet. But big game hunting drew him toward the mountains, and he returned to explore for many years. He also wrote of his experiences in 14 essays for *Forest and Stream*. Grinnell concluded that "The scenery is grand, game plenty, the fishing unexcelled" and offered the nation the first real publicity about Gla-

cier's mountains. Soon other men of wealth journeyed here to hunt, with the Baring family of English bankers, Ralph Pulitzer, and Henry L. Stimson typifying adventurers of that era. Geographical names in Glacier including Singleshot, Fusillade, Gunsight, and Baring are a few mementos left by those hunters.

Prospectors also explored this region, with "Dutch Lui" Meyers being among the first to find a vein of what he described as "grayish white quartz carrying gold, silver, copper, and some lead" in 1889. But getting the mountains opened to legal prospecting took another nine years. Meanwhile, James J. Hill's Great Northern Railway was snaking its way westward. Once surveyor John F. Stevens declared Marias Pass usable, construction proceeded up Summit Creek, across the Continental Divide, and then descended along Bear Creek eventually to parallel the Middle Fork of the Flathead River. Almost overnight, civilization sprouted along the route of Great Northern Railway, which began service in 1891. Travelers came in greater numbers, with a few taking the time to wander toward spots like Lake McDonald. One of those tourists was Dr. Lyman Sperry. A college professor and traveling lecturer, Dr. Sperry was on the lookout for scenic attractions, hoping to add subjects to his lecture list and helping the Great Northern publicize their new route. What enchanted Sperry most was alpine scenery. His interest in glaciers led him to declare that "a man can find anything he wants in this region."

The coming of the railroad introduced a handful of settlers to the western valleys. People like Milo Apgar, Charlie Howe, George Snyder, and a few others carved some homesteads out of the forested shoreline of Lake McDonald. Other hardy pioneers drifted to likely spots further north, especially where meadowlands offered natural fields. Valleys adjacent to the North Fork of the Flathead River soon boasted a few ranches. The settlers around Lake McDonald quickly realized that scenery was one of their most profitable resources. They began to cater to railway travelers, providing meals and cabins and boat rides up the lake. A few acted as guides. An infant "Glacier Hotel" soon appeared at the upper end of the lake near Snyder Creek, later to be

Frank Liebig, one of a handful of robust early-day Forest Rangers who sought to protect Glacier country before it became a park.

expanded and become Lake McDonald Lodge. The tourist business had begun.

Backcountry trails, however, served more than just tourists. Persistent prospectors kept searching for signs of wealth. Some promising veins offered hints of copper. Mineral Creek, far up the McDonald Valley, became the site of early exploration and investment by people like Mrs. Elizabeth Collins, the "Cattle Queen of Montana." And with the eastern slope opened to prospecting in 1898, a flood of excitement and expectation overwhelmed the region. Dozens of claims were filed, many people believing that their strikes would prove as rich as Butte. The settlement of Saint Mary was born in this boom. To the north, in today's Many Glacier

Packing horse at Haunted Lake, Porcupine Ridge in Background about 1907. — Courtesy Glacier Park

area, the town of Altyn claimed its leadership of the Swiftcurrent mining district. Several hundred prospectors pawed at nearby slopes. Exploration shafts were sunk, companies were formed, investment was attracted, a few mines were developed. But yields proved dismal. The boom went bust. Within a year or two most of the miners had left, although a few diehards held on for another decade or more. At the same time, however, the discovery of oil to the north in Alberta and also near Kintla Lake, spurred a bit more excitement. A primitive road was carved through the forests to the Kintla region, with exploration rigs soon to follow. Small deposits of gas and oil also were discovered in the valleys of the eastern slope. But like the dreams of copper and gold, oil proved to be insufficient to sustain investment. Interest in mining and drilling waned and by 1907 it was clear that mineral wealth could not be found.

In addition to railroaders, homesteaders, and prospectors, some people with a less exploitive outlook also discovered these mountains. Besides writers and publicists like Grinnell and Sperry came others intending to protect the region. As part of a national conservation movement, Congress permitted the establishment of forest reserves (later called national forests) in 1891. That same year the Lewis and Clark Forest Reserve was established, which included Glacier's western slope. Glacier's eastern slope would be added after 1898. But in terms of bringing protection or regulation, little changed until 1900. By then forest rangers started patrolling the region. Men like Frank Herrig and Frank Liebig guarded the region against abuses and waste. They fought forest fires, enforced game laws, watched for timber thieves, looked after tourists, and kept the trails open. It was their intent to provide the orderly development and use of the region's resources.

At the same time, a few people believed that mere conservation did not provide enough protection for the scenic treasures of this region. Advocates of the national park idea began gaining influence, especially once the search for minerals proved futile. George Bird Grinnell, one of the most influential spokesmen for the park idea, promoted the cause in a 1901 article for Century Magazine entitled "The Crown of the Continent." He argued that recreational and aesthetic concerns demanded more attention in the form of protection. Men like Grinnell and Sperry helped convince Great Northern Railway officials to support the national park concept for Glacier, a critically and politically important move.

Cutbank Chalets and Cutbank Valley. — Courtesy, Montana Historical Society

On December 11th, 1907, Montana's Senator Thomas H. Carter introduced a bill to create Glacier National Park. Several years of public debate followed. A few local homesteaders feared the loss of their land. Critics of the Great Northern argued that a park would preclude using any of the mountain passes for a competitive railroad route. Some people believed that timber and other park resources — especially wildlife — should be harvested rather than preserved. Nevertheless, those voices of opposition never sounded in unison. And proponents of the park made a few compromises regarding rights of private land owners, valid mineral claims, and water development projects. Compared with other conservation fights, the move to establish Glacier Park was not very controversial. On May 11th, 1910, President William Howard Taft signed the bill creating Glacier National Park.

Right: Stephen Mather, first Superintendent of National Parks who conceived the idea of an over-the-divide road in the park. — Courtesy, Glacier Park
Below: Rising Wolf Camp, 1917. — Courtesy, Montana Historical Society

Builders of a National Playground

Glacier's first superintendent, Major William R. Logan, arrived in August of 1910. He faced a virtual wilderness (just then plagued by a dry summer and forest fires which blackened nearly 50,000 acres within the park). Logan began his work that season by appointing a ranger force of six men. He also surveyed the region, formulating ideas about developing Glacier into a "playground" more acceptable to modern tourists. Working with other national park planners, Logan later proposed building an extensive grid of roadways, a plethora of hotels, and a vast network of trails. Of all his ideas, the "Transmountain Road" concept proved most popular, later to become Going-to-the-Sun Road.

But plans of Superintendent Logan and his successors paled in comparison to the immediate investment and construction initiated by the Great Northern Railway. Between 1910 and 1917, the Great Northern spent $1.5 million developing tourist facilities in Glacier. Nine rustic chalets were constructed at various backcountry locations (with today's Granite Park and Sperry chalets still remaining); three tent camps offered more primitive shelters; and a "Mammoth Mountain" hotel was built at Many Glacier, costing a half million dollars. Belton Chalet (at West Glacier) and Glacier Park Lodge (at Midvale, now East Glacier) rested just outside the park near the railroad's depots. A network of roads and trails were built to link these various accommodations.

A

B

*The automobile age reaches
Glacier Park.
Opposite Page: Dedication of
Going-To-The-Sun Highway, July
15, 1933, at Logan Pass. —
Montana Historical Society.*

*This Page: (A) Two Medicine Chalet
(B) On the road to the summit in July.
(C) Early-day travel still had its
hazards.
(D) Glacier Park Hotel.
All photos courtesy of Montana
Historical Society*

C

D

Over the next two decades, people who visited Glacier followed patterns established by the Great Northern and its hotel company. A majority of tourists arrived by train, disembarking near the large hotel at East Glacier. Riding horses through the park became the primary mode of travel. From East Glacier, trail riders rode to Two Medicine Chalet. From there they headed to Cut Bank Chalet and on to Saint Mary Chalet and Going-to-the-Sun Chalet, and on until the Continental Divide was crossed and the train was reboarded at West Glacier. Lake launches and auto-bus trips offered optional means of approaching scenic areas. And the railroad literature encouraged people to hike as well. At least a week was required to see the park in the manner prescribed for the typical tourist, with some people taking a month or more to "do" Glacier.

That genteel style of tourism, however, was outdated by the building of the Transmountain Road. Once the National Park Service was established, in 1916, funds for such major development projects became available. Surveys conducted in 1917 and 1918 settled the new route across the Continental Divide through Logan Pass. Actual construction took more than a decade and the cost was some $3 million. On July 15th, 1933, Going-to-the-Sun Road was officially opened. It was a highway intended for "the great mass of people" cutting through the heart of the park, and meant to introduce visitors to Glacier's wilderness.

Whether that roadway beckoned people into the backcountry could be questioned. Going-to-the-Sun Road certainly altered the way tourists explored the park. Instead of spending a week or a month winding and wandering along backcountry trails, the "heart" of Glacier could be viewed in a day. Instead of depending upon chalets or tepee camps for food and shelter, campgrounds and motels gained favor. In the years to come, an estimated 95 percent of Glacier's visitors confined their journeys in the park to that narrow ribbon of roadway. And statistics proved that building the road was a popular idea: only 40,000 people toured the park in 1925, but 210,000 people traveled through in 1936. Each year thereafter, with the exception of the World War II era, visitation to Glacier continued to increase. With this influx of people and automobiles, more facilities were added to provide for the new style of vacationing, with campgrounds and picnic areas (and visitor centers by the 1960s) making the scenic roadway more like a corridor of civilization. Meanwhile, the old and disused chalets and tent camps were destroyed or removed. The tempo of a Glacier Park visit grew faster, accommodations were designed for more people and shorter stays. By the late 1960s, one estimate showed the average visitor remained in the Glacier area for 25 hours.

But during the 1960s a preservationist philosophy began to challenge the value of roadways and rapid visits. An awakened interest in and concern for the environment generally led more people to forsake their cars to investigate Glacier's backcountry. More hikers meant more sophisticated management techniques, and restrictions were imposed to preserve what wilderness remained. Adding to that mood, the Wilderness Act of 1964 mandated that vast natural areas within Glacier and other national parks be protected from any further encroachments by civilization. People wanting environmental quality asked probing questions about the preservation of Glacier's unique features. Concern over the purity of the park's air meant monitoring neighboring industries. Realizing the park's water could be polluted led to refurbishing sanitary facilities. Studies of eagles and elk, grizzlies and ground squirrels, natural fire and a host of other ecological concerns helped highlight the fact that Glacier, in 1974, was unique enough to be named one of the World Biosphere Reserves. People slowly rediscovered the fact that Glacier Park was more than just a rapidly passing scene on a cross-country tour. It was a place to be pondered; a place to be preserved and enjoyed.

The call of the mountains changed through the years. The roar of the wind and waterfalls, the whisper of pines and the echoing call of loons gradually mixed with the hoofbeats of Indian ponies and the muffled tread of Indian trackers. The voices of trappers and traders, explorers and exploiters soon mingled with the curses of miners and the laughter of tourists. The mountains called with an almost mystical allure. At times these Rockies offered passage to the plains; beckoned with the temptation of wealth; and stirred the spirit of adventure. In Glacier National Park, the call of the mountains still can be heard.

Above: By the mid-'60s Glacier Park was attracting a million visitors annually, 95 percent of whom saw its vistas by automobile. — Mel Ruder

Opposite Page: Post cards celebrating the west's new playground. — Courtesy Len Eckel.

3003   GOING-TO-THE-SUN CHALETS, GLACIER NATIONAL PARK   5A-H214

8145   SPERRY GLACIER, GLACIER NATIONAL PARK   5A-H213

A Merry Christmas and Happy New Year

TWO MEDICINE LAKE

214   GREETINGS FROM MONTANA

8136   GOING-TO-THE-SUN HIGHWAY, GLACIER NATIONAL PARK   5A-H227

The Ascent of Chief Mountain

by Bert Gildart

In the northeastern corner of Glacier National Park, country that was once the domain of the Blackfeet Indian, there stands a turret-shaped mountain. This geological oddity, on the plains east of the main range, has attracted the attention of explorers and mapmakers from the earliest times. Its existence was first noted on the Arrowsmith maps, published in England in 1796, upon which it was called "King Mountain." Peter Fidler, who supplied the information for these maps, visited this area in 1792, and was the first white man to record this landmark.

Lewis and Clark also saw the mountain from a vantage far to the south and called it Tower Mountain. Once the mountain was referred to as "Kaiser Peak," but none of those names ever stuck. Appropriately, the name is derived from the Blackfeet Indians who have always held it in awe as "Old Chief," "Mountain-of-the-Chief," or simply, "Chief Mountain."

Legend has it that in the early days only one Blackfeet ever attempted to climb the mountain. The attempt was made more than 150 years ago. A hunting party of young men were encamped at its base, and one of the youngest and most ambitious of the young warriors declared that he would go to the summit. His companions watched him from below until he passed out of sight along one of the very highest ledges. Then the spirit of the mountain must have met him, for although the rest of the band waited many dyas, the young warrior never returned. Thereafter, the Blackfeet avoided any close acquaintance with the "Chief."

Perhaps the warrior's wish to climb the mountain was based on his recollection of a Flathead legend the Blackfeet treasured and added to their own.

The story concerns a Flathead warrior, a man watched over by a spirit so mighty that no peril of battle or of the hunt could overcome him. When at last in his old age he came to die, he told the young men his long-kept secret. Many years before, as the time approached for him to go alone into the forest and seek the vision which should be his guide and protection throughout life, he sought a spot and a spirit which had never before been tried. Carrying the usual sacred bison skull for his pillow, he had

crossed the mountains and journeyed east into the far-off Blackfeet country. Then, with none to aid him save the steady power of his own courage, he ventured upon the ledges of the "Chief-of-All-Mountain." There, choking down each gasp of panic when wind and overhanging walls tested his endurance, the warrior finally forced his way up to the very summit. For four days and nights he paced the summit, chanting warrior songs, attempting to make peace with the gods who were to decide his destiny.

It is said the Spirit of the mountain attempted to drive him off the peak during his vigil. On each of the first three nights, with ever increasing violence, the Spirit had come to him and threatened to hurl him off the face of the cliff if he did not go down on the following day. But each time he refused. Instead he spent each day pacing the summit, chanting his warrior song and waving his peace pipe in the air. Finally, on the fourth night, the Spirit yielded, giving him the token of his life. In later years none of the young Flatheads ever dared to follow their great warrior's example, and for almost half a century he remained the only man who had braved the Spirit of the Chief and made it his friend.

The legend might have a basis in fact. In 1891, Henry Stimpson, Secretary of State during the Hoover administration, and Secretary of War during the Franklin Roosevelt administration, journeyed to the Chief Mountain area and felt the challenge of the mountain. Three friends including a full-blooded Blackfeet Indian began their ascent on a blustery summer day. His journals recalls the climb — and their findings!

"Two hundred feet up," wrote Stimpson, "came our first trouble, perhaps the worst of the day. We were sidling along a narrow shelf, with arms outstretched against the wall above, when we reached a spot where the shelf was broken by a round protruding shoulder. Beyond it, the ledge commenced again and seemed to offer our only way upward. I was leading at the time and, after examining it, turned back to a wider portion of the shelf for consulation. It was not a place one would care to try if there was an alternative."

The journal continues, noting the frustration of the party and difficulty they had negotiating the shale rock. Still they plodded on and Stimpson's journal records their progress as they neared the summit.

"Six or seven hundred feet more of steady work, and we could feel the summit breeze beginning to blow down the narrow chimney. Billy, their Black-

feet guide, was then sent to the front, and at half past one, the first Blackfeet Indian stepped out on the Summit of Chief Mountain.

"The summit," wrote Stimpson, "is a long ridge of disintegrated rock flanked at either end by lower rounded turrets, and at its highest part is no wider than a New England stone wall. On the opposite western side the cliffs fell away as on our own, but they seemed shorter, were composed of looser rock, and far down below we could see steep slopes of shale meeting them part way. After we had picked out our various landmarks in the wonderful outlook about us, and I had made my record from compass and barometer, we pushed our way carefully along to the highest point of the narrow ridge, in order to mark it with a cairn of rocks. Just as we reached it, the Indian who was still in the lead, suddenly stopped and pointed to the ground. There, on the very summit of Chief Mountain, safely anchored by rocks from the effect of wind or tempest, lay a small, weather-beaten bison skull. It was certainly one of the very oldest I have ever seen. Even in the pure air of that mountain top it had rotted away until there was little else than the frontal bone and the stubs on which had been the horns. Billy picked it up and handed it to us quietly, saying with perfect conviction, "The old Flathead's pillow!"

Stimpson concludes by noting that they left the skull where they had found it, believing ". . . that the devotion of the old warrior who had brought it was an influence quite sufficient to protect this memorial of his visit."

Today, the 9,056-foot mountain is not so difficult to ascend. By using J. Gordon Edwards' book, A Climber's Guide to Glacier National Park, the challenge of route finding is simplified and, because of a series of dirt roads which have been constructed to the base, a trip up this mountain can be completed in one long day. In fact, rock cairns have been laid out so that in essence there is a marked route all the way to the top. From this vantage many of the park's more spectacular peaks can be seen as well as the plains which stretch beyond the limits of the imagination. Off in this direction can be seen the Sweet Grass Hills and, on a clear day, the Bear Paw Mountains — well over a hundred miles away. Closer, as one looks to the west, Mount Merritt, with Old Sun Glacier covering most of its east face, can be seen. Also to the west can be seen Mount Cleveland which at 10,438 feet is the highest mountain in the park.

Opposite Page: Chief Mountain. — Rick Graetz

by Bert Gildart

Early in the morning Joe Heimes discovered an illegal cache of furs and, after a hurried trip back to his ranger station to alert others in authority, he returned and settled in behind a large fir tree, determined to wait for the poacher's return.

Six hours later the low clouds that had been hanging over the valley floor began to unleash their load. At times there was rain, other times a mixture of snow and rain. Heimes was getting wet and he was growing very cold.

In another two hours Joe was down to his last cigarette, and even on a miserable day in May the mosquitoes in the back-country of Glacier National Park were out in force. Heimes was beginning to get discouraged, afraid the poacher had caught wind of his presence. But Heimes was not one to give up easily, and so he resolved to wait until dark.

Around dusk, Joe's large Malamute dog perked up her ears and emitted a low rumbling growl. Clamping a firm hand over its muzzle and unholstering his pistol, Joe began looking around. Suddenly a large raw-boned man entered camp, taking strides as Joe recalls "like Bigfoot." Then the lanky man took off his pack, laid down his rifle and began nursing the still smoldering fire.

"I was half way to him," recalls Joe, "before he heard me. Then he looked up and grabbed for his gun. But I had him dead in my sights, and I hollered, "You lay your hand on that gun and, by God, I'll shoot you right through the guts!"

The man Heimes had caught on that wet spring day in 1929 was no ordinary poacher. His name was Joe Cosley whose history to that time included the distinction of having been appointed a ranger in 1910 when Glacier was established as a park, being fired several years later for the trapping of furs in the park; a WWI record of having killed 60 Germans as a Canadian sniper, and the notoriety of being able to evade both American and Canadian authorities for almost 20 years. "He was," recalls Heimes from his cabin in Lakeside, Montana, "a mountain man who was every bit the equivalent of Kit Carson or Jim Bridger. Luck was all that enabled me to catch him."

Whether it was luck or not is debatable, for Heimes does not appear to have been a man to trifle with. A ranger for 38 years in Glacier National Park, he retired in 1962. But at 80 his eyes still are piercing, his voice firm, and his hands and back still strong enough to harvest a cord of wood a day, "Though if you want it," says Joe, "it'll cost you $450."

But Joe still considers the apprehension of Cosley luck, and merely a continuation of luck that enabled him to march Cosley out from the back country to the eastern mountain front where the celebrated poacher was quickly brought to trial. "Yes, sir," recalls Heimes, "Cosley had a streak of bad luck for a while but only for a short while. Before we were finished with him, I'd say his shrewdness and good luck were back and in great abundance."

Heimes caught Cosley on May 8th in the Belly River Country of Glacier National Park, a place where winter reluctantly releases its grip on the land. Snow still blanketed the hills and formed white patches across the meadow. "I was preparing for John J. Wes to bring in my spring supplies," recalls Heimes, "and I had to blow a beaver dam which was backing snow melt up over the old wagon road. Wes would come in through Cardston and Mountain View with a Canadian Mounted Police escort in an old wagon and each year the trail flooded for miles. I had to blow that dam away twice a year.

"Well, at any rate, that's when I saw tracks down there in the snow and the sand, and I could see where someone had been looking around for beaver. My dog and I followed a long way and finally we came to a tarp laying over a pole. Inside, there was a hindquarter of beaver, and a muskrat was stuck between his blankets along with several traps. When I saw that we went back to the ranger station at Belly River where I called Tom Whitcraft, the ranger then at Waterton Ranger Station. He wasn't there but the Canadians said they'd tell him he was urgently needed and precisely where I could be found. Then, mighty quick, we hiked the three miles back to the poacher's camp and hid behind a tree.

"As I said, we waited almost ten full hours before he showed and I caught him. But at the time I wasn't sure who I'd caught. I'd never even seen a picture of him before. But I'd heard a description, so when he gave me a fake name I said, 'Well, you sure look more like Joe Cosley to me.'"

Glaring back, he said, 'Well, I'm Joe Cosley all right, but you ain't taking me in.' And then he added, 'Ain't no ranger in this park takin' me in.'

"You know, I might have let him go if he hadn't said that. I didn't want to go to headquarters anyway. I had a dog team and it meant I might be gone a week. It was too much work. And back in those days poaching wasn't a real serious thing. Generally, we'd just take the furs, unload their gun and let them go. As it was, I spent three long days with the man, not to mention what happened after the trial.

"The first night after I caught him we were too far from the station to go back. The woods were thick, and it was almost dark. So we stayed up all night. We just sat there watching each other. And every 15 minutes or so he'd tell me he had to go to the bathroom.

"It was a long night, but finally morning came and Cosley said, 'Well, you might be going but I shore ain't.' I told him then that I'd cut a stick and beat him back to the station, and that just as soon as I finished the smoke he'd given me, we were going.

"That convinced him, but we hadn't gone over 300 feet when all at once he took off running. Never said 'Goodbye' or nothing.

"Well in '29 I wasn't so bad at running myself, so I took off after him and tackled him. Cosley took a few swings but he wasn't really fighting, just more try-

Joe Cosley was born May 24, 1870 aboard the cabin sailboat his French father and Algonquin Indian mother used at the time for commercial fishing in Lake Huron. Early years also included life on a homestead in Ontario, Canada with subsequent moves into various parts of the southwestern part of the U.S. At the age of 25,. records indicate he was living in Kalispell, Montana where he worked as a U.S. Forest Service ranger in what is now Glacier National Park.

In 1910 he was transferred from the forest service to the park service and served as a ranger until he was dismissed for his trapping activities. As Joe Heimes says, "Cosley had one set of rules, the park service another."

Even in his early years an aura of mystery surrounded Cosley, and people liked to spin yarns about him, some based on the truth, some probably not. For instance, Joe had many girl friends, but one returned his $1500 diamond ring to him. Cosley is reputed to have buried the ring in a tree and then told others of this action. For a while there were diamond ring prospectors peeling away new-growth bark in many areas of the park.

Another legend about Cosley concerns his illegal trapping experiences and, once, when two tired rangers were attempting to overtake Cosley, they were surprised when he suddenly appeared from the brush and stated in so many words that he knew they would be tired and would they care to join him for supper, that he served a delicious French stew.

Another time, in what may have been a more characteristic fashion, Cosley stated simply to a ranger, that if he ever caught him on the trail again he'd kill him.

Cosley's career also included a stint in WWI with the Canadian Army where he was subsequently decorated for his skills as a sniper. Today, Glacier honors the man with a namesake: Cosley Lake is located between Belly River Ranger Station and Stoney Indian Pass, one of the most beautiful areas of Glacier National Park.

Cosley's primary source of income, however, was always his trapping, and in this mode he met his demise in September, 1944. At the age of 73 in a wind-swept trapper cabin north of Prince Albert he died alone of scurvy. The last entry into his log reads:

"I am growing weaker. I can hardly write . . . I have reached the end."

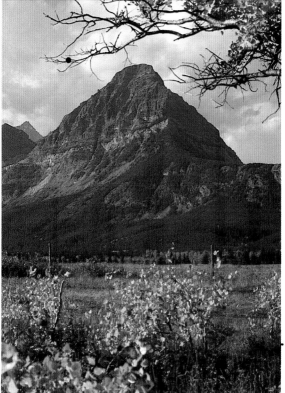

The Cosley namesakes:
Above: Cosley Lake
Right Top: The Cosley tree bearing initials he is presumed to have cut in the '20s. This tree received so much attention by visitors that after it died, the section with his initials was removed and preserved by the park service.
Right: Cosley Ridge above the lake.
Bruce Selyem photos.

ing to get away. Finally, he gave up and said, 'OK, I'll go now.'

"Well, we hadn't gone another 300 feet and I had to make another flying tackle. After wrestling him to the ground he said, 'OK, I'll go.'

"This happened one more time. Only this time he was fighting for keeps; I was afraid he'd kill me. But finally I had the opportunity to take his head and bang it against a tree. Down he went. Then I tied him with the laces of my boots.

"When Cosley came to, he said, 'I can't go; I'm sick.'

"Well, I knew he was sick, damn sick and at that point I didn't know what I was going to do. But just then my dog's ears perked up and along came Tom Whitcraft and the Canadian I'd left the message with. Just like the Seventh Cavalry they were, arriving in the nick of time. We walked the rest of the way back to the station, and we had no more trouble with Cosley that day.

"Next day Tom said he wanted to go back to Waterton and I said the hell with that. You see, Tom was a good looking fellow and," emphasizes Joe with a twinkle in his eye, "a real woman chaser. In fact, that's the reason I couldn't get ahold of him the first day. He was single then and he'd been chasin' a woman. So I said, 'You're going to let me take this bird over Gable Pass by myself? My God. if Cosley gets away then I'm in trouble and you will be too.' That changed his mind!"

For Heimes, the remainder of the trip to court was without incident. A grueling trip on snow shoes over Gable Pass to East Glacier and then, a day later, a train trip to what is now West Glacier. Then the next day a trial, which as Heimes recalls was held about two o'clock in the afternoon. Cosley was fined $100 and given a suspended jail sentence of 90 days. He was then released. And that, reflects Heimes, is when Cosley's usual good luck returned.

"What they should have done is made him spend at least five days in jail. That would have given us a chance to beat him back to look for all those hides he had cached. As it was I went over to a store in Belton (now West Glacier) and store owner Mark Sibley said, 'You know where Cosley is now?' I said, No, and that I didn't give a damn just so long as Cosley stays out of my way, that I wanted to stay out of his way too!

"Mark said, 'Well, he's on his way back to Belly River, and he's just left. He's going to try and beat you guys back to his beaver cache!'

"As soon as I heard that I went to see this fellow up at McDonald Station by the name of Clarence Willy. Willy took right off after Cosley and Willy was a good

Joe Heimes. — Bert Gildart

man, a good strong fellow. He followed Cosley 12 to 15 miles but returned late that night and said that Cosley was a little too good a traveler for him.

"Next morning Tom Whitcraft and I took the train back to East Glacier and then drove a Model T by way of Cardston to the Canadian Belly River Station. From there we had to walk, but we weren't too concerned. It was about 30 miles from the town of Belton to Belly River and today that takes a good strong hiker about two days. And that's if he's on good summer-cleared trails!

"But when we got back to his camp all we found were tracks. During the course of the night, that 59-year-old man had snowshoed up McDonald and Mineral Creeks, crossed over Ahern Pass and removed 40 to 50 beaver blankets and somehow disappeared from the Belly River Country. We couldn't have missed Cosley by more than a few hours. Maybe only minutes. What luck! But to this day you know, I'm not sure whether it was his good luck or my good luck. You see, after that he went north into Canada where I've been told he trapped, wrote old girl friends and became quite a legend.

"But me, I never saw the man again."

Joe Heimes went northeast when he was a young man — from California to Shelby, Montana, riding the rails for the sole purpose of seeing the Jack Dempsey-Tommy Gibbons fight. That was in June of 1923 and, at the time, Heimes was 22 years old.

Heimes stayed for the fight held July 4th and spent much time prior to the fight talking to the two pugilists. His scrapbook contains posed pictures of both Dempsey and Gibbons which Joe took himself.

After the fight, Heimes went to Glacier and, as fate would have it, an appropriate job was waiting for just such a man as Joe. It was the beginning of a career with the park service that lasted until 1962 when he retired as a National Park Service ranger.

Though never married, Heimes has pictures of a number of women in his scrapbook, most of whom, say his friends, were the nicest things you'd ever want to meet. "And they'd ride, walk — even run — to the most remote spots in the park to see him." Today, his companion is a malamute dog that is very much like the one he had with him in the Belly River Country that eventful day of 1929.

Heimes' experiences were varied and fascinating, but the one that received the most publicity is his encounter with Joe Cosley. Currently Heimes is still employed and works as a caretaker near Lakeside, Montana.

Ranger's Notebook

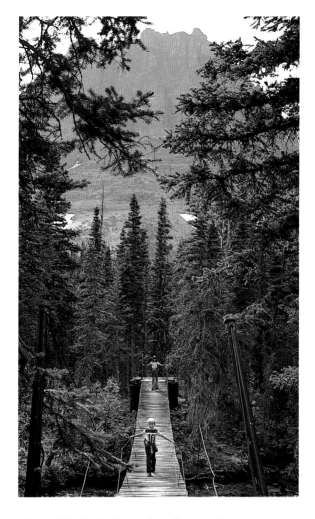

Above: Glacier Park is primarily a trails park. Installation of temporary suspension bridges such as this allows access to backcountry from the thoroughfare of Going-To-The-Sun Road. — Bert Gildart

Right: Along the Highline Trail, looking at Heaven's Peak. — Rick Graetz

by Bert Gildart

"Where can I go now and view nature undisturbed?" — *John James Audubon, 1846.*

Late one evening in Glacier's Belly River country, I watched with a small group of companions as a herd of about 20 elk materialized from the woods and slowly grouped along the stream that ran by our camp. For more than an hour the herd meandered along the bank, stopping here and there to quench their thirst. Now and then a calf would kick up its heels and charge through the water.

Suddenly an old bull lifted his head and flicked his ears back and forth — testing the air and trying to locate sounds that were inaudible to human ears. Then, gradually, we too heard the noise; a sharp crack from the woods that grew louder and louder as the unidentified object moved closer.

The sound of breaking twigs sent the herd galloping across the stream, churning up water as they trotted across the shallows. Then, just as suddenly as they had materialized, they were gone, disappearing into the rapidly descending gloom of night.

Next morning at the crack of dawn, our curiosities aroused, we ambled down to the bank where our elk had been drinking and found tracks made by what appeared from the sign to have been a small black bear. Nothing really dramatic, but, nevertheless, a reminder that we had seen something special —something that one generally sees only in the wilderness.

My companions and I have had many similar experiences in our years of wandering through Glacier's backcountry. Once it was a cow elk swimming across Lincoln Lakes; another time it was a porcupine rubbing its quills along the side of our tent during some wee hour of the morning. The point is that it's still possible, even in the wake of 20th century technology, to enjoy experiences that John James Audubon was searching back in 1846. We can have these opportunities primarily because Congress decreed in 1916 that a number of areas would be set aside as "vignettes of our National Heritage." Because of a superb system of trails, Glacier is one park that offers easy access to its wilderness areas. Venture along one of them and invariably you will return with indelible memories that can be recalled when the need for a lighter moment may occur.

Glacier Trails

Visitors arriving in Glacier for the first time often find it disconcerting as they begin their attempt to plan a backcountry trip into the park. Their dilemma is understandable; most of the park's trails are one-way trails that leave hikers miles from their point of origin. There are, however, several trails that traverse some of the most superb country the park has to offer without leaving one stranded at the end. These are the park's loop trails, and several will be described. Additionally, two other excursions will be described that could round out the hiker's appreciation of the park. For easy access, all areas will be named according to their point of origin. But prior to embarking on any of these treks, a few points should be kept in mind.

All of the following hikes are strenuous ones. They should not be attempted by anyone who is not in good physical condition. Water from a known clean source should be carried or stoves should be packed so that water can be boiled. Additionally, in most areas fires are not permitted, necessitating the possession of a good backpack stove. Because special park regulations may apply and the number permitted into these backcountry areas at any one time is limited, it is mandatory for hikers first to register at either a visitor center or a ranger station.

1. Packer's Roost — This 32-mile, three- to four-day round trip hike offers special views of the peaks of the Lewis and Livingstone ranges. In midsummer a pageant of wildflowers greets the hiker. So might grizzly and black bears. This is prime habitat for bears as well as for goats, marmots, pikas and deer, the latter of which may wander through your campground.

The trail begins at Packer's Roost. Two miles later it crosses McDonald Creek via a suspension bridge which is usually in place by the first week in June. Several miles later the trail climbs 1,800 feet at which point one reaches the heights of Flattop Mountain. A campground is located here along the west bank of Flattop Creek. Additionally, as with many park campgrounds, a privy, food cache pole and hitchrack are available. Because of the steep climb, it is recommended hikers spend their first night here.

The distance from Flattop Mountain to Fifty Mountain is 12 miles. The trip continues along Flattop Mountain with very little gain in elevation. At the north end of Flattop Mountain, the trail drops 600 feet into the Kipp Creek Drainage, then climbs abruptly to the Fifty Mountain Campground, located in one of the most beautiful sections of the entire park.

From Fifty Mountain one returns along the Highline Trail, so named because it generally maintains an elevation above timberline. From the campground it is a distance of 12 miles to Granite Park Chalet, one of the park's two such backcountry "hotels." If reservations to spend the night have been made, the amenities offered are worth the cost. Naturalist talks are given in the evening, and occasionally one can see bears from the balcony. If the $35 to $40 cost is prohibitive, hikers are still welcome to refresh themselves by purchasing tea, kool-aid or some other nonalcoholic beverage.

Near the chalet, a campground is located, and if you choose to stay here, the next day you must hike a total of about seven miles — virtually all down hill — to return to your point of origin.

Opposite Page: Along the Highline Trail — west side of the Continental Divide. — Rick Graetz
Above: From Granite Park Chalet — Rick Graetz

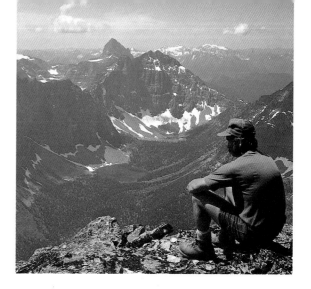

2. Two Medicine Campground

2. Two Medicine Campground — A strenuous 17.4 mile round trip that is best enjoyed by allowing two or three days. The suggested route for this hike is in a clockwise direction starting from Two Medicine Lake and continuing to Pitamakan Pass. This trail may not be open until early July. Because of the precipitous nature of the trail between Dawson and Pitamakan passes, horses are not permitted; persons suffering from acrophobia should beware.

In addition to unsurpassed panoramic views offered by the lofty passes, other features of this area include abundant opportunities to see goats and sheep. In the lower elevations bears are occasionally seen. From the trail near Pitamakan Pass, two small lakes at the head of Cut Bank Valley are visible. Frozen over until mid-summer, they are dotted with icebergs which may linger in the mountain's shadows throughout the course of the summer. Two backcountry campsites are present and are located adjacent to lakes that at times offer excellent opportunities for the fisherman. One of these is No Name Lake, the other Oldman Lake. Again, because wood fires are not permitted, a backpack stove is essential.

Opposite Page: 50 Mountain is the designation for a park-like plateau near Flattop Mountain. — Bruce Selyem

Top Left: Rising Wolf Mountain, 9,505 feet, with a halo of clouds seen from Two Medicine Valley. — Gordon Sullivan

Top Right: Hiker atop Mount Rockwell southwest of the Two Medicine Valley, Mount Saint Nicholas in the distance. — Bruce Selyem

Bottom: View from Cut Bank Pass to the east. — Gordon Sullivan

3. Bowman Lake — A strenuous 13-mile round trip that can be broken up by camping at either Lower Quartz Lake or Quartz Lake. Anglers should try for cutthroat and dolly varden trout. The hike passes through a dense forest, and this is one of the main reasons for venturing into this drainage. Still, from Quartz Lake there are excellent views of Vulture Peak, which straddles the Continental Divide. A quartz vein on Vulture Peak at the headwaters of Quartz Creek contains a small vein of copper ore which stimulated a bit of unsuccessful prospecting after its discovery in 1876.

Again, this is prime grizzly bear habitat so proper disposal of trash and fish entrails is essential.

Hikers interested in this trip should be prepared to negotiate wet and boggy spots. They should also be in good shape. The trail climbs 1,100 feet over Quartz Ridge, then drops to Lower Quartz Lake. There is another 1,000-foot climb over Cerulean Ridge returning from Middle Quartz Lake to Bowman Lake.

Opposite Page: Two Medicine Lake with beargrass, which is not a grass, but a lilly, and is not eaten by bears. — Alan Carey

Right: Bowman Lake. — Gordon Sullivan

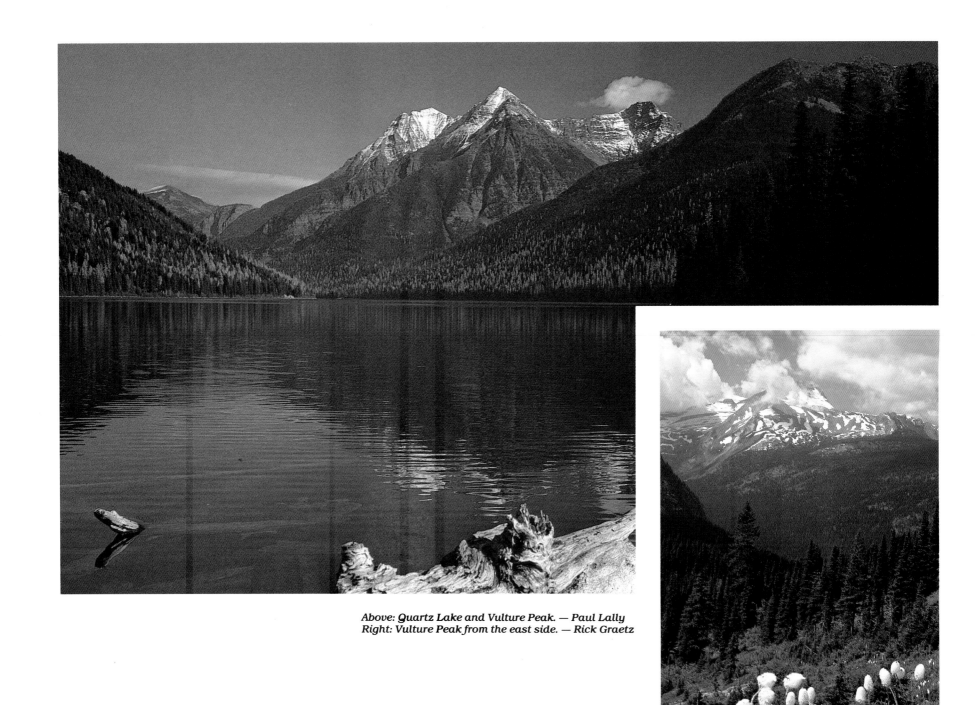

Above: Quartz Lake and Vulture Peak. — Paul Lally
Right: Vulture Peak from the east side. — Rick Graetz

4. Grinnell Glacier exhibit near Appekunny Creek

— This is a round trip that will leave you only two miles from your car when the trail terminates at the Many Glacier Campground store. The total length of the trip is about 25 miles depending on whether the recommended side trip is included in your hiking itinerary. Highlights of this trip include fishing for arctic grayling at both Poia and Elizabeth lakes and for rainbow trout at Kennedy Creek.

At one time the trail over Red Gap Pass was the direct connection with the Belly River area before the completion of Ptarmigan Tunnel in 1931. Today this trail joins with the trail from Ptarmigan Tunnel at a point about two miles from Elizabeth Lake. Dropping down into this lake is well worth the time; the scenery is spectacular and the fishing at times can be excellent.

Two camp areas are located along this route, one at Poia Lake, the other at both the foot and head of Elizabeth Lake. Fires are permitted at both campsites though it is often difficult to obtain wood. Only wood that is dead and down can be used, so again it is advisable to carry a stove.

Recommended time for this trip is three days. The trail is steep and rises 2,700 feet to reach Red Gap Pass. Just prior to reaching the pass one must negotiate a series of extremely steep switchbacks. There

Top: Mount Wilbur from Altyn Peak. Peter and Alice Bengeyfield

Bottom: Elizabeth Lake. — Bruce Selyem

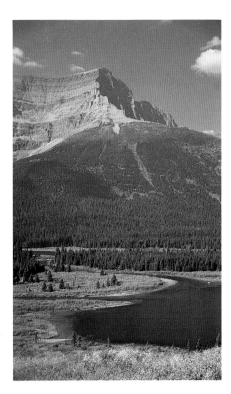

5. Swiftcurrent Campstore — This roundtrip hike traverses a route that is an historic one in the annals of the park.

Historically the route is referred to as the North Circle route and was initiated in 1915 by W. N. Noffsinger, an attorney from Kalispell, who began the Park Saddle Horse Company. Under the —X6 (Bar X Six) brand, the company expanded until it owned more than 1,000 head of horses, making it the largest saddle horse outfit of its kind in the world. Each year the company handled more than 10,000 park visitors and did so successfully until World War II. After the war, the "discovery" of the Going-To-The-Sun Highway by a more affluent car-owning American society brought an end to the saddle-horse business.

The North Circle trip, one of the company's most popular, required five days, with stops at tent camps or chalets. Today, the following suggested route is identical to the one traversed by riders bouncing along on Bar X Six stock between 1915 and 1942.

Begin your trip at the Swiftcurrent Lodge located in the Many Glacier Valley. Stops may include overnight camping at Elizabeth Lake, Belly River, Cosley Lake, Stoney Indian Lake, Goat Haunt, Fifty Mountain and Granite Park Chalet. On the last day you will hike over Swiftcurrent Pass, traveling beneath the Swiftcurrent fire lookout prior to concluding your trip some four to seven days later back at Swiftcurrent Lodge.

This trip is an arduous one, but it passes through the heart of the park and crosses the Continental Divide several times. Excellent fishing is offered along the way for several species of trout and arctic grayling.

Left Top: Swiftcurrent Point from Wilbur Creek. — Gordon Sullivan
Left Bottom: Glenns Lake. — Bruce Selyem
Above: Mount Cleveland, Kootenai Lake. — Gordon Sullivan

54

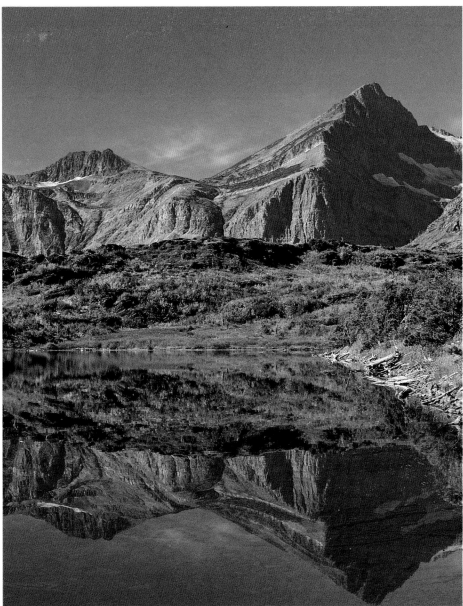

Left: Mount Merritt (with glacier) from above the Belly River Drainage. — Rick Graetz
Above: Red Rock Lake. — Gordon Sullivan

is a similar drop in elevation to Elizabeth Lake which includes another series of switchbacks.

The climb from Elizabeth Lake to Ptarmigan Tunnell is 2,300 feet. From the tunnell the trail is downhill all the way to Swiftcurrent Campstore. Backpacks could be left here (at owner's risk), while hikers trudge the last two miles along the paved road back to their car.

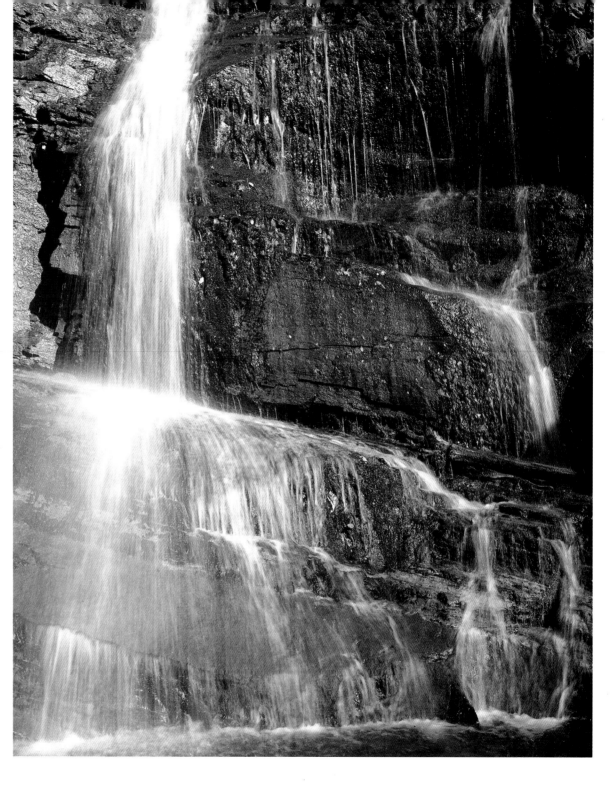

Above: Apekunny Falls. — Peter and Alice Bengeyfield.
Right: Unidentified falls in Ptarmigan Creek. — Gordon Sullivan

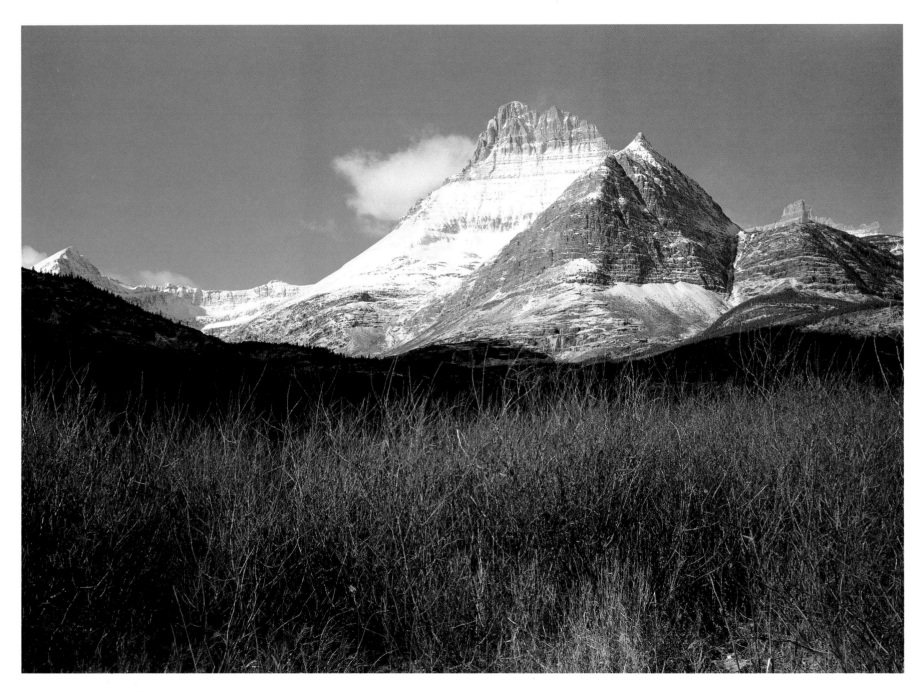

Mount Wilbur from Swiftcurrent Creek. — Gordon
Sullivan

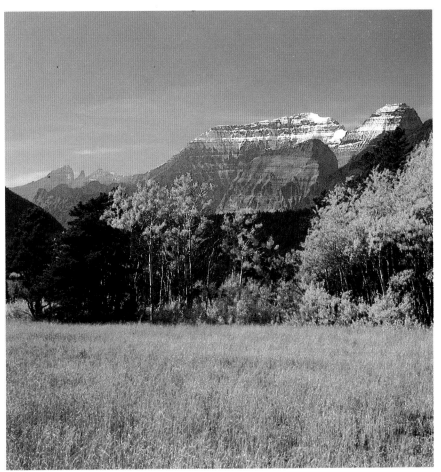

Left: Cathedral Peak from Glenns Lake. — Bruce Selyem
Right: Mount Cleveland from the Belly River Ranger Station. — Bruce Selyem

Opposite Page: View from Chief Mountain toward Mount Cleveland and the Belly River drainage. —Rick Graetz

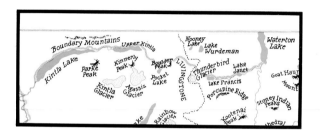

6. Goat Haunt to Lower Kintla Lake

6. Goat Haunt to Lower Kintla Lake — This 32-mile, one-way hike is one of the most rewarding trips for the experienced backpacker. It offers a variety of terrain and traverses deep, forested valleys, lakes, glacial cirques, and two mountain passes. Because the trail passes through all the park's vegetative zones, the opportunity exists to see virtually all species of park wildlife.

Boulder Pass is the highest of the two passes. Less than 50 years ago the basin on the east side of the Pass was filled by the massive Boulder Glacier. Today only small patches of ice on the north slopes of Boulder Peak remain. Still, striated rocks, sharp moraines and melted lakes abound, providing mute testimony to glacial activity.

Subalpine larch, the Glacier Park tree, also is found in this vicinity, and, appropriately, its presence also is associated with the recent glacial activity. Look for these interesting trees near Boulder Pass. They are characterized by needles that grow 20 to 40 in a bundle and may measure between 1 to 2 inches. Unlike most conifers, needles of this tree are shed in the fall. The altitudinal range of this species serves as the best distinction from its close relative, the western larch. Subalpine larch grows only in partially sheltered areas at or near treeline, many hundreds of feet above the uppermost limits

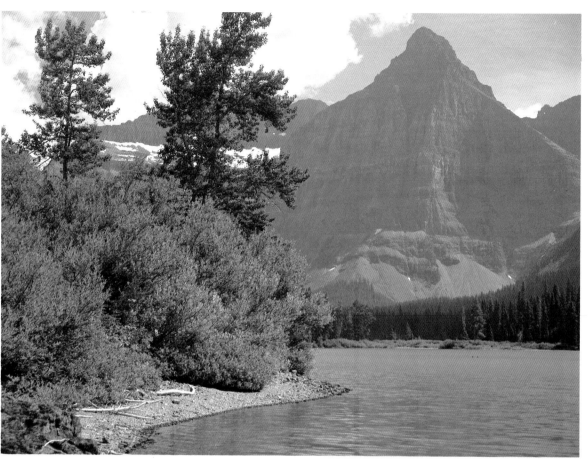

Francis Lake. — Gordon Sullivan

of western larch. This, and the wooly character of the new branch shoots, are the most reliable distinguishing features.

In some years there will be snow on or along the trail throughout the summer, particularly in the vicinity of Boulder Pass. Because the trail in this area passes over much rock and scree, hikers should be alert for rock cairns that mark the way.

After leaving the Boulder Pass area the trail drops sharply into the Kintla Valley where it winds through luxuriant growths of cow-parsnip and thimbleberry. These plants can make hiking difficult — particularly on a wet day. As a result, foul-weather gear is highly recommended.

A number of campgrounds are placed along the entire route, but, if possible, an attempt should be made to spend one night at the Hole-in-the-Wall Campground. Because of surrounding waterfalls, the location is particularly enchanting.

The only drawback of the entire trip is logistics. Transportation must be arranged, as Kintla Lake Campground lies at the end of an unimproved dirt road — well over 150 miles from Goat Haunt. Nevertheless, the drive takes you through several remote and historical sections of the park, providing additional intrigue to the overall trip. As a last resort, rest up and retrace your steps. As with all of Glacier's trails, repeating a hike invariably offers a new set of experiences.

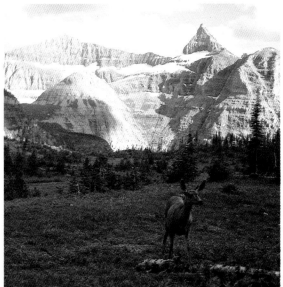

Above: At west-side base of Browns Pass. — Gordon
Sullivan
Right Top: Wurdeman and Nooney Lakes — Bruce Selyem
Right Bottom: Thunderbird Peak and visitor. — Bruce
Selyem

61

Above: Above Thunderbird Pond, Browns Pass area.
— Gordon Sullivan
Right: From the top of Browns Pass. — Gordon
Sullivan

Above Left: Bowman Lake. — Bruce Selyem
Above Right: Pocket Lake from Boulder Pass. — Peter and Alice Bengeyfield
Left: Abandoned cabin at head of Bowman Lake. — Bruce Selyem

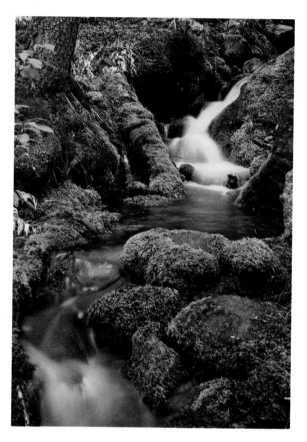

Above: Thunderbird Mountain from Hole-In-The-Wall. Peter and Alice Bengeyfield
Right Top: Unidentified falls at Kintla Lake. — Peter and Alice Bengeyfield
Right Bottom: Kintla Lake. — Bruce Selyem

7. Valleys of Southwest Glacier Park — The

southwest corner of the park is wilderness in the
true sense of the word. It can be thought of as an
extension of the Great Bear Wilderness to the south.
Although trails do exist, they receive only inter-
mittent maintenance, if they receive it at all. The
route east through Nyack Creek across Cut Bank,
Dawson and other passes is historic as well as
scenic. It was much frequented by Indians traveling
to and from buffalo country.

Hikers have an additional measure of freedom in
this area. Although permits are required, as they are
throughout the park, backpackers are not confined
to designated campgrounds.

Hiking is strenuous at certain times of the year
because of damp, thick, brushy undergrowth. Also,
this is bear country, harboring some of the animals
that have gained a reputation for breaking into
cabins along the North Fork of the Flathead.

No specific hikes are outlined here since routes
are easy to identify up the Lincoln, Harrison, Nyack,
Coal, Park and Ole Creek drainages.

Lake McDonald by the season.
— All photos, Paul Lally

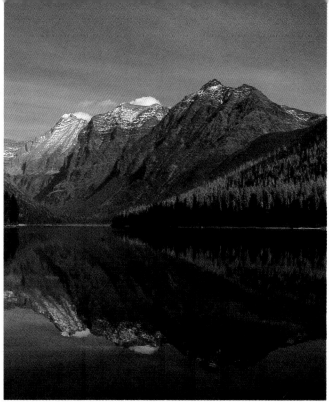

Top Left: Eagle Ribs Mountain from Firebrand Pass. — Dave and Janet Panebaker
Top Right: Harrison Lake. — Bruce Selyem
Bottom Left: Mount Stimson, Razoredge viewed from the east at Milk River Ridge. — Bruce Selyem
Bottom Right: Park Creek, Two Medicine Pass from Scalplock. — Dave and Janet Panebaker
Opposite Page: Mount Saint Nicholas from U.S. Highway 2. — Bruce Selyem

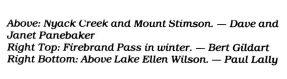

Above: Nyack Creek and Mount Stimson. — Dave and Janet Panebaker
Right Top: Firebrand Pass in winter. — Bert Gildart
Right Bottom: Above Lake Ellen Wilson. — Paul Lally

Ski-Tours in Glacier Park

Virgin snow lay all around as we skied down the gentle slope of a winding trail and glided slowly onto the white mantle covering Josephine Lake. Here, my partner and I were reminded of the first commandment for all skiers in Glacier National Park, "Be thou alert to change."

Several minutes later, as we rested in the middle of one of the Park's frozen waterways, we noticed that the temperature was rising fast. Every gust of wind now seemed to carry an ominous message: Mother Nature was not to be calmed!

Half an hour ago, the cold wind had still been intense enough to drive a throbbing pain into our heads. Now, well past the center of the lake, it was too warm to ski wrapped in our down parkas. Our thermometer indicated the temperature was beginning to stabilize near 40 degrees, an increase of more than 45 degrees in the past two hours from the overnight low of minus five.

After we made the far shore, we began changing wax, and, as we did, we watched the wind whipping snow between our feet and off the surrounding mountain peaks, snow which was not yet compacted by the warm sun and wind.

Then, Mother Nature growled!

Along the far ridge a dull roar began that soon filled the air. The mountains seemed to groan from every direction with such vehemence that it was difficult to audibly locate the exact source of the disturbance. Sight, however, was not deceived and, from Grinnell Peak, large slabs of snow could be seen sliding down the peak and out onto Josephine Lake where we had just labored. Huge boulders were cascading down the slope; dwarfed trees were being upended. Then just as quickly as it began, all motion ceased, the roar abated, and gusts at Josephine Lake were again audible.

Top: Two Medicine Pass, Mount Saint Nicholas in the background. — Dave and Janet Panebaker
Bottom: Making esses down the east side of Two Medicine Pass. — Dave and Janet Panebaker

Philosophizing as much to myself as to my accompanying seasonal park ranger Fred Reese, I said, "Fred, for once we chose the right path!"

Every year in some part of the country including Glacier Park, winter enthusiasts are killed or maimed for life, because of an unfamiliarity with their surroundings. It need not be so.

An appreciation of the snow conditions found in Glacier, an understanding of winter trails, or a realistic analysis of one's skills could have averted disaster. At any rate, such knowledge can enable the winter skier to prepare adequately for a most unique tour through Glacier during quite possibly the most fascinating season of all.

Unstable weather conditions, a prime contributor to avalanches, are not at all uncommon in Glacier. At times, temperatures may plummet to 20 or 30 below and then, several days later, warm winds or "chinooks" may send the mercury soaring into the 40s or even higher, all in the course of several hours. The result is unstable snow conditions, which precipitate numerous avalanches throughout the park. The important thing, then, is to know how to recognize the danger signs.

In some areas of the country, the Forest Service is helping those interested by offering free courses in snow study. Prior to skiing in Glacier, take one — if possible — otherwise, write a Forest Service office such as the one located at the Federal Building, Missoula, Montana 59801 and ask for the brochure on snow avalanches. Study this pamphlet thoroughly. If you follow its cautions, you should be able to avoid dangerous situations.

Unstable snow conditions also produce complicated and uncommon waxing problems. This situation contrasts with areas such as Yellowstone, where temperatures are consistently cold and ski-tourers almost can manage on one or two types of wax.

In Glacier, waxing gear should run almost the entire gamut. Thus your pack should include the klisters, and a small torch to remove this messy paste should temperatures suddenly drop. Many have found waxing to be such a chore that they rely on skins for climbing and for "kick" over flat terrain. A downhill wax then serves for any coasting that is to be done.

Because many of the trails over which you may wish to ski in Glacier are steep and narrow, and often prove difficult to negotiate, it may be in your best interest to remove your skis and carry them over these areas. To permit freedom of motion for your arms, a backpack or rucksack that has at-tachments for packing skis is a real convenience. If you slip, your hands are free for recovery; your skis are secure and won't slip away as you reach to regain balance.

Because the terrain in Glacier can be rough on equipment, one precautionary measure that should be taken is to include a spare tip and extra cable, especially for trips longer than just a few miles. If you are accompanied by other skiers — as you should be for safety's sake — and, if you are using the same brand of equipment, a smaller number of total spare parts may be carried by the entire group. This practice is used by patrol rangers and should not be overlooked, as you would testify had you ever floundered back through several feet of powder with a broken binding.

Prudence dictates investigating local weather reports at park headquarters. Some skiers even include a small, transistorized radio for trail-side forecasts. The weather man is often wrong, which is understandable when talking about an area whose weather is determined by coastal and continental weather fronts and huge elevation differences. If he predicted "blue skies and light zephyrs ahead" better prepare for a white-out or a prolonged blizzard. Should you be in the back-country at such an inopportune time, it would be wise not to travel. Better to lose time and remain snug in your sturdy mountain tent than to risk fatigue, hypothermia, or the prospect of stumbling off a cliff. Prepare for such a stop-over by including extra food, enough for two or three days.

If you are caught in a sudden storm or plan to camp above timberline, you will appreciate having a self-supporting tent. Locating logs in high-country to serve as an anchor or "deadman" for tent ropes and pegs is an impossibility, and snow depth is so great that pegs are ineffective.

With the thousands of miles of trails available during the summer, one of the most difficult decisions to be made by the winter vagabond is where to go in this 1,538-square-mile park. Further complicating matters is the fact that a number of summer highways now remain unplowed and provide excellent opportunities to see Glacier by ski during the winter. In one such unplowed area, for instance, Fred Reese and I encountered a mountain lion which had been following a herd of elk. The story of its stalk lived on in the snow. But not all roads will provide this wonderful opportunity. In some areas, snowmobilers have free rein.

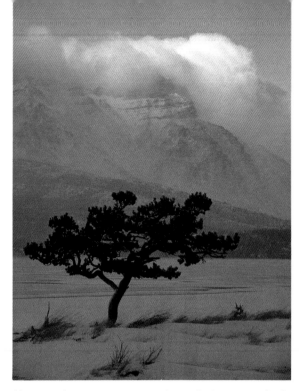

Above: Saint Mary Lake area in a wind storm typical of the east side of the park in winter. — Gordon Sullivan
Below: Frozen air bubbles on a beaver pond in Saint Mary Valley. — Bruce Selyem

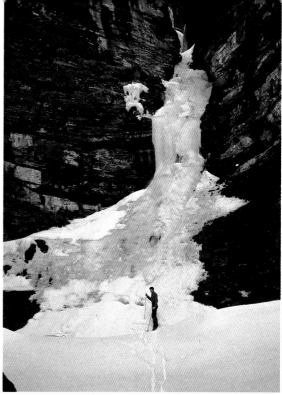

Left: Granite Park Chalet Snowbound. — Bruce Selyem
Above: Pacific Falls locked up for the season. — Dave and Janet Panebaker

Avalanche Lake — Perhaps one of the most rewarding short jaunts is to Avalanche Lake, located west of the Continental Divide. To reach your starting point, drive along the Going-to-the-Sun Highway around Lake McDonald until you come to the unplowed section. Now, continue along this famed highway — but on skis — for about the next four miles depending on how far the road has been plowed. Soon, if you do not spend too much time photographing frozen McDonald Falls, you will come to Avalanche Campground. Avalanche Lake is then two and a half miles straight up a winding trail. At times, even skins won't provide a firm grip and you will have to remove your skis. But the view of the gorge is worth the effort, and there is always

the opportunity to observe deer and elk. The area is also one of the few within the park in which I have seen mountain lions.

Because this lake, which is always frozen during the winter, is located in a lofty cirque, the surrounding mountains often are shrouded by clouds. If you would make this a two-day winter trip and camp at the lake, your chances should be good of intimately viewing the wilderness surrounding this frozen expanse. Regardless of the number of days duration, skiing time, depending on conditions, is about eight hours.

Many Glacier — East of the Continental Divide, the probability of finding clear skies is better. One excel-

lent trip that could conceivably be made in two days is to ski into the Many Glacier Area. Three to five days would make a more relaxed and enjoyable trip. To reach the Many Glacier area, drive from the town of Babb, Montana to the Many Glacier entrance station. At this point, if the road is unplowed — to be expected — you will then have to ski 10 miles along a flat surface to reach Many Glacier. Once there, you will have an unexcelled opportunity to photograph bighorn sheep. This is the wintering area for these mountain monarchs, and in November and December you probably will see and *hear* them as they collide with one another and shatter the silence locked in this immense valley.

View up the Coal Creek drainage from Gary Lookout.
— Bruce Selyem

Josephine, Grinnell Lakes, Advanced Trips —
Another excellent ski-tour in the Many Glacier area is to Josephine and Grinnell lakes. You will find the trailhead for this trip near the end of Swiftcurrent Lake. Round-trip time will require about five hours, but skiing across these lakes to view snow plumes trailing away from lofty mountain peaks is well worth the energy expended; it will long be one of my most memorable experiences.

There are other parts of the park that I would also recommend for their unique beauty. Accessibility, however, is more difficult, and advice on entrance into these areas is best obtained locally. Prior to your arrival, order a topographical map from the Glacier Park Historical Society and then discuss one of the following treks with a park ranger.

From near Chief Mountain to Belly River and Elizabeth Lake; from St. Mary to Red Eagle Lake; from Summit, between East Glacier and Walton Ranger Station, out Autumn Creek; and from the Loop, above Avalanche Campground, to Granite Park Chalet. This last route is best attempted in May, after the main road has been partially opened.

Just as in the two areas previously discussed, avalanche danger in these latter basins does not constitute a major hazard. By using common sense,
all these trails are suitable for any who are in good physical condition and have a reasonable knowledge of how to camp during the winter.

Glacier's Heartland, Waterton to Packer's Roost
—There is one final area that I would recommend, but it is made with some reservation. This trek is a minor odyssey and should not be attempted unless you have a sophisticated knowledge of winter survival, are in excellent physical condition and have plenty of time.

On this trip, you will ski through the very heart of the park where some of the loftiest mountains in Montana serve as sentinels. Here, as you leave the valleys behind and approach one of the summits, you will find no other sign of life, save perhaps a ptarmigan or a gaping hole left in the snow by a startled grouse that had been seeking relief from the biting wind. This area, as some have said, is truly the "Crown of the Continent," but it is also a region that welcomes no one.

Prior to leaving, analyze your skills objectively, and by all means, go well out of your way to avoid slopes which even hint at avalanche potential. In December of 1970 six men lost their lives in a snow slide while attempting a winter assault on nearby Mt. Cleveland, Glacier's highest peak.

To begin this trip through Glacier's heartland, which is best made between January and April, drive to Waterton townsite in Canada where you should advise one of the Canadian park wardens (rangers) of your intentions. Generally, you may say that you route will take you around Waterton Lake, down Waterton Valley and then up several thousand feet to Fifty Mountain. From here you will want to cut across country passing over Flattop Mountain, dropping into the Mineral Creek drainage and coming out finally near Packer's Roost. Allow about five days to cover this trek of approximately 35 miles.

Return transportation to Canada, or to the foot of McDonald Lake if you decide to reverse the route, will have to be arranged in advance. Usually this necessitates either renting a car or arriving with your companions in two vehicles.

Logistics, though, are a minor problem; your greatest difficulty will be selecting one of the almost equally enticing areas through which to ski. But whichever you choose, prepare properly and, upon completion, you'll be fit to try another route . . . and another.

Well, why not?

Time is in your favor, for in many years you can ski-tour Glacier for almost nine full months.

Left Top: Grinnell Glacier. — Gordon Sullivan
Left Bottom: Along McDonald Creek from the
Avalanche Creek Campground. — Gordon Sullivan
Above: From Mount Henkel to Mount Wilbur and
Swiftcurrent Pass. — Gordon Sullivan

Question:
How do you tell the difference between a grizzly bear and a black bear?

Answer:
Kick the bear in the rump and climb a tree. If the bear climbs up after you, it's a black bear. If it knocks the tree down, it's a grizzly.

— *Very early bear research method*

One feature that immediately separates black bears and grizzly bears is their temperament. Where one is inclined to be docile, the other is aggressive. Where one retreats, the other advances. And where one climbs trees, the other charges. Paleontologists tell us that it is this skill — the ability to climb trees — that accounts for their dispositions.

From fossil remains it is believed that grizzly bears first emerged about one million years ago. *Ursus americanus,* or our now relatively retiring black bear, preceded the grizzly by about another one million years. Both animals, however, evolved from one common ancestral species, *Ursus etruscus,* with subsequent environmental factors shaping the two distinct personalities.

Ursus etruscus originally lived in Asia where it was essentially an inhabitant of the forest. But climatic changes required some bears to evolve into an animal of the tundra to cope with the lack of cover. No longer could the tundra bear retreat from danger by taking to the trees or protect its offspring by sending them into high branches. Instead, to survive attacks from other predators, it became more aggressive. On the treeless prairie, sows were forced to aggressively defend their cubs. Assisting her were genetic and evolutionary adaptations such as long claws (useless for climbing trees) and a large physical stature. Huge back muscles evolved for digging up sod in search of underground-dwelling rodents and the roots, tubers and bulbs of plants associated with the plains. Those same back muscles make up the prominent shoulder hump of the modern grizzly.

Where black bear sows retreated, *Ursus arctos,* the evolved grizzly, advanced, and this characteristic was firmly imprinted on the cubs. Not surpris-

Ursus Arctos Horribilis — The Grizzly — For the big bear to survive the park must manage pressure on back-country habitat that bears share only grudgingly with hikers. — Alan Carey

ingly, most grizzly bear attacks today involve mothers with their cubs.

The black bear preceded the grizzly to North America, across the periodic land bridge connecting America and Asia by almost 250,000 years.

Today, the grizzly bear is the largest carnivore in North America. Its family includes the big brown, giant Alaska and the Barren Ground bears. The very largest of these are found in southwestern Alaska, on Kodiak Island. Bears have been killed there that measured nine feet two inches from the tip of their noses to the end of their short tails. One taken on Kodiak Island weighed an incredible 1,656 pounds. In Glacier, bears are not nearly this big — the largest averaging about 600 pounds.

Despite its enormous bulk, the grizzly is surprisingly agile. On the straightaway, bears are fast and have great endurance. A grizzly in Yellowstone Park, running ahead of an automobile, was clocked at thirty miles an hour.

Bears gorge themselves all fall and attain their greatest weight in October just before their long winter sleep.

Bears do not hibernate, although they do den up and spend the winter in a lethargic sleep. The bears usually dig their winter dens in early fall. Most of the dens are dug on north-facing slopes, beneath big tree roots at high elevations. With the onset of the season's first big snowstorm, bears retire to their dens and sleep.

During this long winter sleep, a bear's body temperature drops six to eight degrees, and its heartbeat and breath rate slow down markedly. Unlike the true hibernators, the bear easily can be awakened.

Most bears in Glacier come out of hibernation in April. Shortly after emerging bears are active, and if food is scarce they lose much of their excess body weight. This is the time they break into cabins in the North Fork country of Glacier Park.

Bears breed in June, and at such times, the males fight viciously for possession of the female. When dominance has been established and the lesser bear has been driven from the area, the two become very playful. Their courtship lasts for a week or more. After mating, the male wanders off to seek another receptive female.

Cubs are born in January, while the female is in the winter den. Twins are usual, but triplets are common, and occasionally quadruplets occur. At birth the cubs are covered with short gray hair, and their eyes and ears are sealed. The grizzly cub is 8 to 10 inches long and weighs from eight ounces to one pound. During the course of its life a cub may multiply its weight 1600 times or more to become the unquestioned ruler of the mountains.

Mother bears are strict disciplinarians. The cub that does not heed its mother's command is given a swat that sends it sprawling. The cubs stay with their mother until they are two years old, which means that most females breed only every third year.

Grizzlies rarely climb trees, even as cubs. After a year or two, the claws lose so much of their curvature that they are not efficient hooks for digging into tree trunks. But there are always exceptions. A bear climbed high into a tree after several hikers near Elizabeth Lake in September of 1980.

How dangerous is the grizzly to man? Occasionally human beings are terribly mauled or killed by these bears. The bodies are seldom eaten, but there are exceptions to this too, and 1980 marked another one of those rare incidents. Again at Elizabeth Lake the flesh and bones of a bear's victim — the park's

Elizabeth Lake — scenic and lovely here — is difficult to imagine as the site of one of the park's six fatal bear maulings. — Rick Graetz

Evolution of a Bear Management Program

Following Glacier's first bear-caused deaths in 1967, it became clear that the park needed a written plan to help prevent future maulings. In 1968 such a plan was instituted. In essence the plan was designed to separate people and bears.

Initially, all backcountry camp sites were policed for garbage — the primary contributor to the 1967 deaths. Additionally, another portion of the plan prescribed that anyone who sees a bear report the observation to a park official. This information is recorded, noting such facts as the time and location of the bear sighting, the bear's color and size, and its apparent disposition. If several reports of an aggressive bear begin to accumulate, an investigation is made.

As part of the evolving plan, a number of well trained rangers were organized into a group referred to as the Bear Management Team. This group of about ten people received training in tranquilizing bears with a dart containing a needle-pointed syringe propelled from a gun accurate to a range of about 50 yards.

A tranquilized bear can be checked for age, sex, condition and can be blood tested and tagged in relative safety.

Another aspect of the Bear Management Plan requires that regular patrols be conducted by rangers in their respective areas. Backcountry rangers are alert for signs of bears — scats paw prints, and churned-up sod, which indicates that bears have been digging for roots and small mammals.

If such signs are observed a more thorough investigation is initiated, attempting to assess the extent of the bear's activities and where they are concentrated. In most instances, trails are posted advising hikers of the bear's presence. If a bear is sighted, a report is filed with the communications center.

sixth mauling fatality — were virtually consumed. Still, this type of behavior is rare, according to Dr. Charles Jonkel, who has been studying grizzlies in and around Glacier. "In fact," says Jonkel, "statistically bear maulings are rare, particularly when one considers the large number of people using the park's backcountry." Jonkel cautions that bears are very much like humans. "Each and every one is an individual and, therefore, is unpredictable. This means hikers can't be sure of what to expect from a grizzly. If it sees a person in the distance, it usually will avoid him. But if the bear is surprised up close or if it sees a threat to itself or its cubs, it isn't going to cower. It didn't evolve that way."

Long-time Glacier hikers consider the chance of encountering a grizzly to be one of the risks they assume when they go into wild country. "But," says Glacier's Supervisory Research Biologist Clifford Martinka, "many other people aren't so tolerant. Most humans aren't able to mentally accept what you have to put up with when you have grizzlies around."

And so there are fewer and fewer grizzlies around, for as Martinka notes, "The grizzly is the type of animal that just can't take human pressure. And its problems today are essentially an indication of excessive human pressure — not just on the animal, but on its entire ecosystem."

For a number of years the Bear Management Plan appeared to be working. But in 1976 a girl was killed in a car campground located in the heart of the populated Many Glacier Valley. A problem other than garbage was recognized: the inevitable contact between bears and people produces a potentially lethal condition called in official jargon, "habituation." From 1950 to 1976 the number of people visiting the park annually swelled from 500,000 to almost 1.5 million. Compound this with the approximately 20,000 people who registered for permission to use Glacier National Park's backcountry overnight campsites each summer, and add to that the hordes of daytime hikers, and the stage is set for reinforcing "habituation."

Says Glacier's chief biologist Clifford Martinka, "Who knows how often hikers pass within feet of a grizzly and never know the bear is present? From such repeated contacts and close association, bears soon learn there is no reason to fear people." The danger is compounded every time a bear gets into an unattended backpack. "In this situation," says Martinka, "bears find an easy meal and this meal is associated with the odor of people which lingers on their backpacks."

Historically one of the park's biggest problems has been the association of bears with garbage. In the summer of 1980 two of the three people mauled in Glacier were killed by a bear with traits similar to those involved in the 1967 deaths. This animal had become accustomed to feeding on the garbage easily available in the St. Mary townsite. These problems were considered by the boards that convened following the three tragic deaths of 1980. Glacier's basic Bear Management Plan was modified again, primarily on the basis of the board's findings. The following 1980 modifications provide some indication of the current status of the Bear Management Plan and what the public can now expect from the park:

● "Glacier National Park should continue its present bear monitoring system that allows management to identify and respond to potential people/bear problems. The park should continue to seek ways to improve the system's effectiveness in serving as an alert to park management of potential problems that may be occurring both inside and adjacent to the park.

● "Glacier Park should take the lead in resolving the local sanitation situation and approach the Blackfeet, the Bureau of Indian Affairs, the appropriate departments of the State of Montana, Glacier County and St. Mary community in an attempt to

Some 35 bear-man incidents have been recorded in Glacier National Park, six resulting in fatalities, and all of those have occurred since 1967, in the decade that Glacier Park visitation reached more than a million annually.

Bear attacks grab headlines, but they should be kept in perspective. The first person killed in Glacier Park was struck by falling ice at Blackfoot Glacier. According to a recent park study by Jerry DeSanto, of 156 fatalities in the park from 1913 to 1981, 43 visitors drowned and 33 persons died from falls. Thus some 49 percent of glacier's fatalities resulted from accidents near water or on steep hills and cliffs. Bear attacks account for 3 percent of Glacier's fatalities, compared to 12 percent for heart attacks and 11 percent for vehicle accidents.

Alan Carey photo.

eliminate sanitation practices that are conducive to attracting grizzly bears into close association with people.

"All refuse disposal sites near Glacier Park should be evaluated for their potential for similar habituations of bears leading to other incidents.

● "The board feels the time has come to clearly state in literature used by Glacier Park that the potential for death from bears, even though slight, does exist. The park staff should review its literature with a view toward stepping up its impact on the park visitor and employee."

● Glacier was advised to reevaluate what constitutes a problem bear. Previously, overly aggressive behavior was necessary before a bear was considered a problem. Now the park is preparing to take a harder line on any bear that has torn up camps, consumed other than natural food, or simply become overly familiar with humans. The boards advised that such bears be trapped and immediately removed.

Left Top: Many people think that bears are hungriest and most irritable in the spring after their winter sleep, but most bear-man confrontations occur in the summer as bears lose their fear of frequently observed hikers. — Bert Gildart

Left Bottom: Idyllic Bowman Lake and even populous Saind Mary Lake, Above Right are not too pretty to have had bear-man problems. — Gordon Sullivan, Rick Graetz

• The board also suggested that the availability of natural food for the grizzlies should be evaluated periodically. The belief is predicated upon the assumption that bears tend to be more troublesome when food stress exists.

• It was advised that the transplant program of the Bear Management Plan be improved. It is believed that if it were necessary to capture a bear, the animal would probably be one which was troublesome enough to seriously question whether it should be transplanted within the park. Preferably, other agencies should take the bear, but if this is not possible, the bear should be destroyed.

This advice was given with knowledge that the grizzly bear population in Glacier National Park appears to be stable. From 1967 to 1980 the park had killed 15 bears for management purposes — or an average of slightly more than one a year. Since 1980, although the average number of bears killed has not increased, the average number of bears removed from the park's ecosystem has increased. According to Oak Blair, one of Glacier's Bear Managers, "It is our goal now to remove bears before they get into trouble. We want to preserve within the bear the integrity of its wildness." The result of this conservative approach has resulted in the death of only one grizzly, though at least six bears have been removed from the Glacier ecosystem. Several of these were accepted by the British Columbia Fish & Game Department.

With but one exception then all of the board's recommendations were accepted. The one exception is that the park will not officially insist backpackers be accompanied by another hiker. (Gordon, the man killed at Elizabeth Lake in September of 1980, had been a lone hiker.) Park officials, however, still strongly recommend against hikers going into the backcountry alone.

The Natural World

by Bert Gildart (except as noted)

Glacier Park Mini-Climate

by Bob Frauson

Glacier National Park makes its own weather (micro climate) due to its location straddling the Continental Divide. The predominant weather influence is the flow of moist, warm air from the Pacific which loses heat as it rises over the passes and mountains that make up the west slope of the Continental Divide. Moisture is lost in the lower elevations as rain. Rain turns to snow as the air cools over the mountains. This same cool air then plunges down the eastern slope gaining speed and warming to become a chinook wind.

Cold fronts from the arctic flow down over the east front range from Siberia, Alaska and through Alberta, forcing their way under the warmer Pacific air. This front may be visible as fog or clouds that form at the contact point and even lightning may occur from violent frontal clashes. Large arctic fronts tend to spill over the passes (Logan, Marias, etc.) and flow down into western valleys filling these valleys with cold air, which is trapped under the warm overriding air flowing east. This warm air plummets down the east slope as chinooks and can create winds gusting in excess of 100 m.p.h. In such storms it is difficult to keep the rotating cups on anemometers, as they turn so fast that centrifugal force destroys them.

North winds, which are not winds as such, are the result of a constant pressure of chilling air moving south at from 5 to 10 m.p.h. Elk herds in winter tend to move into these north storms and have been known to move as far as 8 miles in one night, leaving the confines of the park.

Cloud formations that signal weather changes are altocirrus clouds (mares' tails) moving in from the west. They usually precede storms from the west. Lenticular clouds (lens shaped) denote high winds from the west. These transform into a chinook arch that can extend from horizon to horizon. In fall and winter, clouds can shroud the Continental Divide and its peaks for days on end. At other times hat-like "cap clouds" settle on the major peaks.

It can snow in Glacier Park any month of the year. Sometimes snow closes Logan Pass as early as the second week in July. One can usually count on a snow storm on Logan Pass the third or fourth week of August, followed by a beautiful Indian summer. Snow that falls in the western valleys is likely to be moister than east slope snow. The rate of snowfall is a good indicator of avalanche danger. If it exceeds one inch per hour, winter travelers in mountainous terrain must beware. White-outs or ground blizzards can occur at any time, even many days after a snowfall, when there is a strong wind and loose snow. Orientation is difficult under these conditions. A friend once described the difficulty of skiing in a white-out as "like skiing inside a ping-pong ball."

Snow in the last four years on the east front of the park has been light, with accumulations of as little as 74 inches compared to 330 at St. Mary in the late 1960s.

Temperature ranges are extreme and can change very rapidly. One may start on an afternoon cross-country ski trip from Hudson Bay Divide to St. Mary (7-plus miles) in 25 below zero weather with beautiful gliding conditions only to have the temperature rise to 45 above with rain. The snow becomes as sticky as mashed potatoes. Temperatures can stay in the minus 25 to minus 35 temperatures range for a week or so at a time. It sometimes dips to minus 50. Goats are good barometers of such weather fluctuations. Note their position on the mountain side. If they are high on the slopes, the weather will be good; when they are low, watch out!

Most of the large lakes in the park are very deep so that a great deal of cooling of the water has to occur before ice can form on the surface. Lake McDonald seldom freezes over in the winter. Yet east-side lakes may freeze over by Thanksgiving. When the large lakes do freeze, one can hear constant booming in the valleys caused by cracking ice. Wind also affects a lake's ice formation. On a calm, cool night the lake may freeze over. Then a wind might spring up to break the ice and send it grinding down the lake. Years ago on just such an occasion an elk herd went out onto St. Mary Lake on a night when the ice was not safe. Coyotes were out on the ice harassing the elk and the herd milled around in a small group. This concentration of the weight caused the ice to break and about 40 elk drowned in a spot no larger than 30 feet by 30 feet.

An old Indian by the name of Alanzo Skunk Cap told me his method of forecasting a winter. He said to watch where the muskrats build their houses. If they are at the edge of the pond, it will be an easy winter. If the houses are in the middle of the pond, it will be a hard winter. Alanzo passed away a few years ago, but when I pass the ponds near his house I always watch where the muskrat houses are.

Opposite Page: (A) View from one of the many potholes along the slopes bordering the east side of Glacier Park. Note the distinctive lenticular clouds prevalent in Glacier's eastern skies. — Bert Gildart (B) Fall in the Cut Bank Valley. — Bert Gildart (C) Snows and fog come early in the high country. This is an early autumn shot of Heaven's Peak across McDonald Valley. — Paul Lally (D) Battling weather systems high above Glacier Park often release their energy dramatically. — Jeff Workman

A

B

C

D

Editor's note: What follows are profiles of plants and animals that typify the natural communities in which they are found. Certainly any of these living things is interesting in itself, but each can be seen as representative of those plants and animals subjected to common conditions in the habitat. At the same time, these are the "critters" and "green things" visitors often ask about that make Glacier the unusual natural treasure that it is.

Alpine Community:

The alpine community is perhaps the most spectacular, with its annual display of wildflowers. It is characterized by only a few species of trees such as the arctic willow, birch, and fir. A number of mammals, including the pika, marmot, wolverine, and mountain goat, have made interesting adaptations to this harshest of parkland environments. Deer use this area as a summer home.

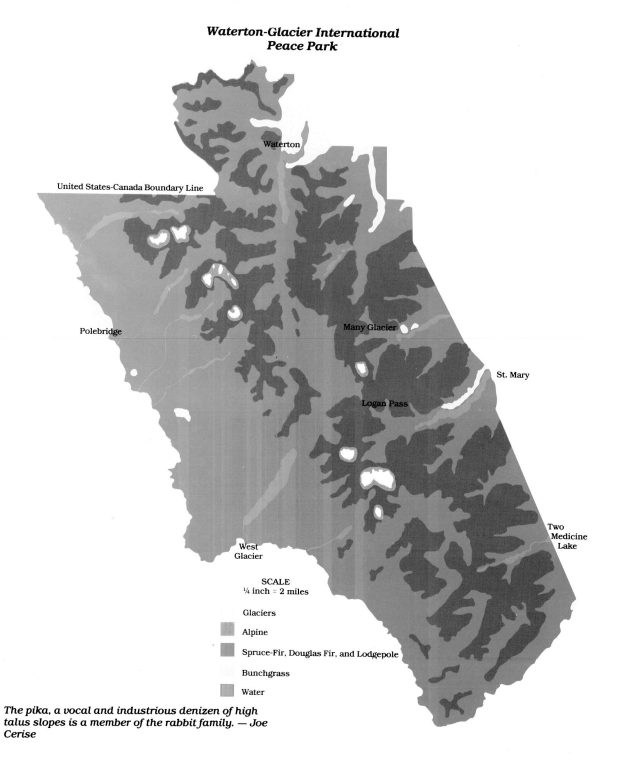

Waterton-Glacier International Peace Park

Waterton

United States-Canada Boundary Line

Polebridge

Many Glacier

St. Mary

Logan Pass

West Glacier

Two Medicine Lake

SCALE
¼ inch = 2 miles

Glaciers

Alpine

Spruce-Fir, Douglas Fir, and Lodgepole

Bunchgrass

Water

The pika, a vocal and industrious denizen of high talus slopes is a member of the rabbit family. — Joe Cerise

A

B

The Ptarmigan

Hard, wind-blown snow comes early in the high peaks of the Rocky Mountain range. It drives the elk down into the low country; it covers the boulder strewn home of the mouse-like pika; and it sends the powerful grizzly bear scurrying to its den for a long winter's nap. In fact, the rugged alpine country forces just about every type of creature to leave or hide. But always there remains a beautiful little one-pound bird — the ptarmigan.

I met this strange bird while crosscountry skiing with a ranger friend in Glacier National Park. At the time it was five degrees below zero and the wind was howling across the vast treeless flat. Both of us were bundled in heavy down coats, warm leather mittens, and thick wooly long johns. All around us the snowy world through which we plodded seemed a mighty deserted place. But suddenly, not more than a half-dozen paces away, were six balls of puffed-up feathers. They were pure white, as white as the snow over which we traveled. It seemed a miracle that we had

C

D

(A) Subalpine fir, foreground, is one of the hardy survivors at the lower edge of the alpine ecosystem. — Jeff Gnass
(B) Hoary marmot, a friendly — sometimes too friendly — alpine animal. — Bruce Selyem
(C) Ptarmigans are about the only creatures to be seen stirring in the winter in the alpine country. — Peter and Alice Bengeyfield
(D) Marmot with a "catch" of jerky. — Gordon Sullivan

not passed them by. Perhaps the flutter of their wings as they scooted deeper into the snow attracted our attention or maybe it was the black of their eyes and beaks that contrasted so sharply with the endless snow. We wanted a better look and so we moved closer, trying not to startle them. But we need not have worried; fear was not part of their nature, and they only returned our stares as if to say, "Any creature out in this weather must be just another ptarmigan."

Ptarmigans are unusual birds. So well have they learned to live with their environment that for years we humans have been trying to copy their survival techniques. But thinking back now on those six birds "bathing" in the snow sends a chill through me, and I'll have to admit that I question how far we have come toward mastering their skills.

If you have heard of the ptarmigan before, you probably thought it a resident of the Arctic or Alaskan tundra. But in some of the mountain regions of our western states, one of the three Northern American kinds, the white-tailed ptarmigan, is often found.

The ptarmigan is a close relative of the grouse. The white-tailed ptarmigan has the scientific name *Lagopus leucurus.* In simple translation of Latin its first name, *Lagopus,* means "rabbit foot." During the winter all ptarmigans grow long stiff feathers over their feet. Their feet do look a lot like rabbit feet. They can walk right on top of soft, fluffy snow where I, even on my snowshoes or skis, often sink deep. On their own "snowshoes" ptarmigans easily make their way in search of willows, birches, and alders which usually have twigs sticking up above the snow.

Ptarmigan chicks are born in June in the arctic-alpine community, where it is still very cold. Unlike many other birds, ptarmigans are born already covered with soft, warm feathers. And a baby ptarmigan is up scratching around in just an hour. One week later, it is testing its wings.

Even with this head start, the life of a ptarmigan chick is not such as easy one. It must be on the lookout for such predators as the hawk, weasel, and wolverine and other inhabitants of the arctic-alpine community. Fortunately, nature has provided a camouflage for all seasons. In summer the feathers of young and adults alike are a blend of brown and white. So well do they fit in with the rocks and boulders that an occasional hiker is seriously startled when a lichen-covered "rock" sails off into the blue, cackling and beating the air as it goes.

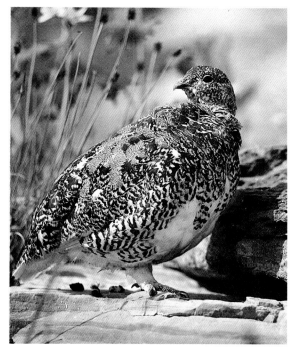

To me the most beautiful coloration occurs in the winter. Then the white-tailed ptarmigan is all white. Its close relatives, the willow and rock ptarmigan, however, retain small areas of black. For years biologists thought the gradual replacement of feathers and the seasonal changes in color were regulated by differences in temperature. Carefully controlled laboratory experiments, however, have shown that it is the seasonal changes in day length that regulate the color of the ptarmigan.

Feathers not only help the ptarmigan blend with its surroundings but also provide excellent protection from the cold. During the winter, the ptarmigan fluffs up its feathers, creating "dead" air spaces that help trap the heat produced by its body. We do much the same thing by shaking quilts and sleeping bags that are filled with feathers.

The ptarmigan conserves heat by taking advantage of the insulating qualities of the snow. Ptarmigans make their caves by diving into the snow and scratching out a hollow, or by pressing their bodies into the soft powder and then merely letting the wind pack drifts of snow around them. Outside these snow "rooms" the wind may be 40 degrees below zero, but inside it is relatively calm and cozy.

If the snow is soft, ptarmigans can wander around underneath where they may feed on buried twigs. Sometimes, if snow becomes crusty on top, these birds become trapped in ice chambers where they may die.

A friend of mine once heard such an unfortunate bird clucking softly beneath him underneath an icy crust of snow. Kneeling down, he took the tip of his ski pole and carefully chipped away at the ice. Suddenly, with a furious beat of its wings, the trapped bird broke into the air and sailed away on a gust of wind. "Maybe we'll see that one again," said my surprised friend. That happy thought sent us sliding off with the same wind that had taken our freedom-bound ptarmigan.

Ptarmigans in summer "trim." Top, John Winnie, Jr.; Bottom. — Gordon Sullivan

Spruce-Fir and Douglas Fir:

These two communities are treated together as they are interspersed with one another from about 4,000 to 7,000 feet. Also, there are only a few mammals that prefer one of these areas over the other. Soil conditions and slope direction are two of the factors that determine which one of the two communities dominate. Look for Douglas fir on southerly slopes and spruce and fir on the north-facing slopes. These communities are home for furbearers and many of the large mammals.

B

C

A

D

(A) Virginia Falls near Saint Mary Lake courses through typical fir forest. — Bruce Selyem
(B) Mule deer use the forest fringe for protection. — Gordon Sullivan
(C) Badger, carnivor of the forest understory and eastern slopes. — Paul Lally
(D) Wildflowers in splendid profusion. — Peter and Alice Bengeyfield

A

B

C

D

(A) Bull moose, enjoying its feast of watery growth, usually seeks protection in stream-side forests. — Paul Lally
(B) Black bear foraging. — Bert Gildart
(C) Glacier Park is thought to be travelled by occasional wolves moving down from Canadian wildlands. — Paul Lally
(D) A rarely observed resident of the forest, the mountain lion. — Bert Gildart

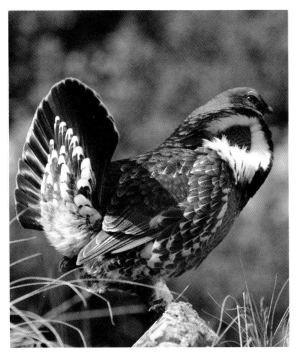

Top: Spruce grouse, not to be confused with the blue grouse, Bottom, has a distinctive red comb over each eye, whereas the blue grouse shows an orange comb and is lighter in color and generally larger than his cousin of the deep spruce forest. The spruce grouse's tameness had led to its rather easy destruction and thus the nickname, fool hen. — Bruce Selyem, Alan Carey

Spruce Grouse

Hikers passing through the spruce-fir community of Glacier park often are surprised by a mottled dark gray or brown bird with a conspicuous black face, throat and chest patch or bib which demonstrates absolutely no fear of the hiker's approach. Upon seeing the bird, hikers are further surprised to find that if they walk toward it, the bird may do nothing more than circle a nearby tree. If charged, the bird may fly to an overhanging branch, but seldom will it ever fly away, though they do possess excellent powers of flight. Spruce grouse apparently feel so secure in the depths of their surroundings that some don't even feel intimidated when approached to within arm's length. There are documented cases of people who have reached out and plucked the bird off its perch. Because of this total lack of fear, this wilderness grouse has earned the name "fool hen."

Other than a lack of fear the ritualistic courtship of the spruce grouse is probably the bird's most interesting habit. These displays can be seen in Glacier's North Fork country in April. The male spruce grouse displays for the female and proclaims his territorial rights with his "drumming". With the female in attendance, the male flies to the top of a tall spruce, performing an aerial display of wing beats and color patches.

There are several variations of the spruce grouse's drumming procedure. Instead of flying out of the top of the tree, as do other grouse, the male may fly from the limb of one tree to the limb of a nearby tree, fluttering his wings and drumming as he goes. Descending to the ground he may pass back and forth from tree to tree, performing all the way down. At other times, the male may fly repeatedly straight up in the air without landing in any tree, displaying while he is descending.

Yet another variation has been recorded where the spruce grouse flies and hops up an inclined tree, drumming as it goes. Near the thicker branches at the top of the tree, the grouse flies to the ground, only to start up again.

When the male spruce grouse is on the ground, he displays and struts for the female like a miniature tom turkey. His feathers are ruffled so that they stand on end; the head is held up and back. The tail, the grouse's glory, is fanned out to its very fullest and raised almost vertically. Hikers encountering a male spruce grouse spreading its splendid glistening tail in a sunlit opening among the pines will know they have entered the depths of the park.

The spruce grouse is well named, for it prefers to live in and around spruce trees, whose needles provide one of its staple foods. Other requirements are abundant huckleberry plants, insects for the young, a sparse ground covering and an arrangement of trees in such a way that openings of a few hundred square feet are common. A spruce grouse could ask for little more in life, except perhaps a little peace and quiet.

What do spruce grouse contribute to the overall welfare of the forest? Because spruce trees give up some of their needles to spruce grouse their overall growth might be infinitesimally faster without the grouse. Huckleberries might produce better without spruce grouse removing their leaves and flowers, but fruits were meant to be eaten so that their seeds may be dispersed after passing through an animal's digestive system. So spruce grouse probably help huckleberries more than they hurt them.

In some small way spruce grouse may help increase the rate of turnover of nutrients in their habitat and thereby increase the amount of life their surroundings can support. Conifer needles are broken down in their digestive tracts and returned to the soil in the form of droppings, dead spruce grouse, the excretions of an animal that has eaten a spruce grouse, or the carcass of such an animal. In some favorite winter haunts spruce grouse droppings may be so abundant that they increase plant growth.

The spruce grouse as a vegetarian concentrates and converts plant material into protein and fats of its body. Other inhabitants or visitors of the spruce-fur community, such as the goshawk, great horned owl, red fox, and coyote are all somewhat better off for the presence of the spruce grouse, but none of those predators depends primarily on the spruce grouse as a source of protein. Thus it seems that the role of the spruce grouse in the broad scheme of life is a minor one, and that the world could go on without it. Still, the thought that the "fool hen" has not yet learned the fear of man means there are places yet to see that retain the vestiges of wildness.

A

B

Lodgepole-Larch Community:

This area indicates frequent and severe burning and is particularly noticeable along Camas Creek Road and in the Apgar region. It is a successional community that will ultimately lead to spruce-fir or cedar-hemlock communities. Elk are common in this area.

(A) Porcupine. — Paul Lally
(B, C) Elk, one of the few large mammals that regularly brave "doghair pine" of lodgepole stands. — Gordon Sullivan
(D) Lupine appears in newly cleared areas such as burns which in turn will likely become lodgepole stands. — Bert Gildart

C

D

(A) Burned area in the McDonald Valley. — Paul Lally
(B) Chipmunk. Gordon Sullivan
(C) Pearlyeverlasting with visitor. — Gordon Sullivan

87

Tamarack

Tamaracks, as they have since the beginning of tamaracks, change color each fall and blaze like bronze flames. When they do, people inevitably look at the species — intermingled with the green of its common associate, the lodgepole pine — and wonder why the hillside is full of dying trees?

Tamaracks are one of the exceptions to the rule that members of the family *Pinacea* retain their leaves or needles. Another exception is the bald cypress that proliferates in the Everglades of Florida. Tamaracks then are properly designated as deciduous conifers; they shed their needles in the fall and stand naked through the winter. But before the needles fall, they turn the most beautiful bronze-tan color imaginable. Next spring the tamaracks will come to blossom; the female flowers with scarlet scales and the male flowers bright yellow: tiny blossoms with delicate colors that seem almost out of place. A few weeks later they will shimmer with new light-green needles.

New spring needles help differentiate them from those of the other needled trees. The needles are from one to two inches in length and occur in bundles of about 15 to 30, growing along the length of the small branchlets. The cones are small, yellowish-brown, about an inch long, with thin, flexible scales.

Such spring delicacy could be achieved only by a tree as tough and sturdy as a tamarack, which grows farther north than any other tree in North America. It also grows in New England. But it is essentially a northern tree and its finest groves are to be found north of the Great Lakes. In the north it thrives in the boglands, but in the northern Rockies it grows on rocky ridges too.

Tamaracks are also known as hackmatack and larch, and in most areas of Montana it is called buckskin, possibly because of the bright tan color of its bark. Hackmatack and tamarack probably stem from Indian words, but nobody seems to have traced them to their source.

Western larch is a prolific seeder and is a close competitor of the lodgepole pine at seeding burned-over areas. The tall, thick-barked mature larches often withstand the heat of forest fires, and, if soil conditions are favorable, will seed heavily in the vicinity of the surviving trees. This situation can be seen in several places on the western side of the park. One notable area is the northwestern side of Quartz Ridge near the foot of Bowman Lake.

Tamaracks are often sought out by fire-wood gatherers in the fall. Wood from dead buckskins

splits easily, readily creating a cheery glow in the hearth, and providing warmth on a cold Montana evening. Weathered buckskins also provide sites for cavity-nesting birds. One old spiraling tamarack was found to be a home for 12 species of birds and 20 nesting pairs, all at the same time. Glacier National Park naturalist, Dr. Riley McClellan, recommended several years ago to forest service personnel that a few snags, such as tamarack buckskins, be marked and left standing until toppled by wind and erosion. Standing, dead trees provide ecological harmony to the forest and create warmth and security for a many of our avian migrants that inhabit the lodgepole-larch community.

A

B

Cedar-Hemlock Community:

A rather small area confined to the McDonald drainage of Glacier National Park and dependent upon large quantities of moisture, this community extends from 3,100 feet to about 4,000 feet. White-tail deer, moose, and red squirrels are occasionally seen here.

Opposite Page: The tamarack or western larch, the only conifer in western forests to change color and shed its needles, gives the forest landscape golden accents in the fall. — Gordon Sullivan photos.

This Page: (A) Red cedar trees flourish in one spot in Glacier Park at the head of Lake McDonald. — Gordon Sullivan

(B) Whitetail deer may be found in cedar-hemlock forests. — George Wuerthner

Plants of the cedar forest floor, (C) Trillium and (D) Bunchberry dogwood. — Bert Gildart

C

D

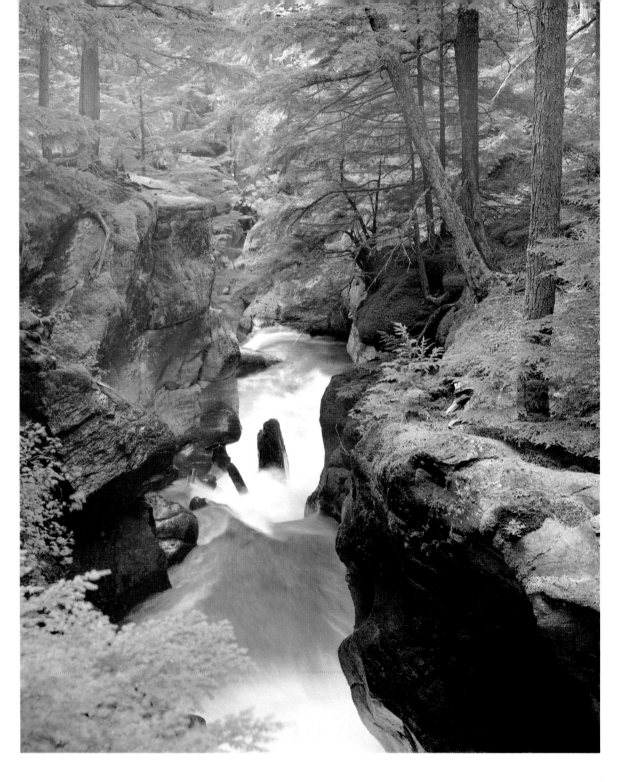

Avalanche Creek, shown here at Avalanche Point, cuts through western red cedar stands. — Bert Gildart

Cedar and Hemlock

The red cedar in Glacier is restricted primarily to an area between Avalanche Campground and the shoreline bordering the upper end of McDonald Lake. Here, a few trees reach great dimensions with a few specimens obtaining heights of 220 feet and measuring seven feet in diameter. Prior to 1910, this community extended over a larger area. But the intense fire of that season eliminated even this thick-barked tree.

The McDonald Valley is ideal for the growth of this particular tree. In this part of the park rain and snow are abundant, and the humidity is relatively high. Two ridges, Howe and Snyder, flank the valley, and keep the McDonald drainage fairly cool.

Western red cedar is not important to wildlife, except possibly to provide cover for the deer, squirrels, grouse, and smaller birds that frequent the area. The seed of this species often are bypassed in preference to the larger cones of nearby conifers.

Cedar was used extensively by Indians over much of the northwest. The trunk was used for canoes and lodges, while the strong, tough inner bark was made into baskets.

Cedars begin their life cycle in mid-April by producing flowers. As the season progresses the fruits or cones mature and, in late August, seeds are shed. These slow-growing trees may begin to produce flowers and fruits at about 20 years of age, but the peak seed crops are not produced until 70 to 80 years of age and continue for 100 to 200 years. As with other species of cedar, a heavy seed crop is produced about every three years.

Growing in close association with the red cedar is the western hemlock. It too is confined to the same area defined by climatic and topographic conditions. Frequently the two species are confused. To differentiate between the two species look at the needles. Those of the cedar are fern-like and may overlap one another; those of the hemlock are blunt. Also look at the tip of two mature specimens. On the western hemlock the tip droops to form a "leader," while the tip of the cedar stands erect.

Bunchgrass Community:

Although scattered sites of bunchgrass and its associated vegetation range up to 6,000 feet, this community is generally confined to elevations below 5,000 feet. East of the Continental Divide this area can be recognized by its prairie appearance and stands of cottonwood and aspen. Areas between St. Mary and Rising Sun along the Going- to-the -Sun Road are typical of this community. Some of the mammals that historically inhabited this area are the bison, muskrat, badger, elk, and coyote.

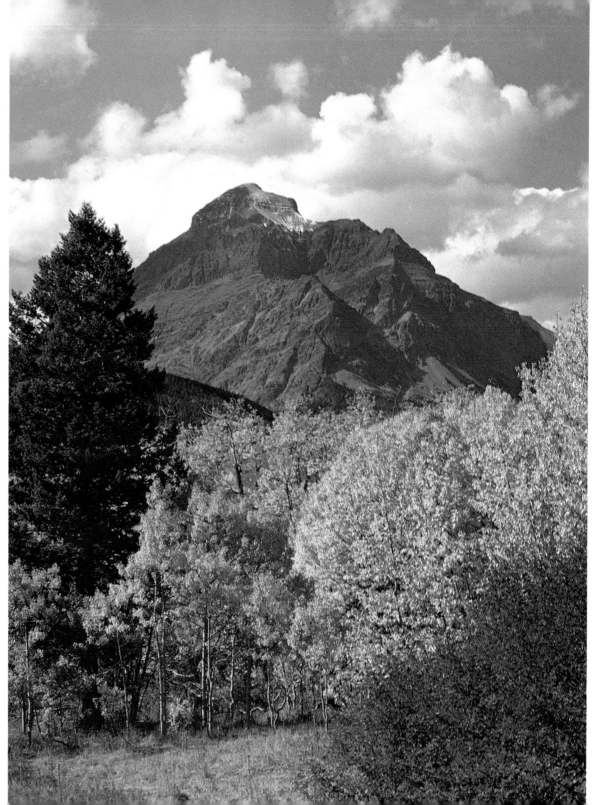

Right: Aspen and cottonwood are part of the bunchgrass community. Rising Wolf Mountain is in the background. — Paul Lally
Above: Golden eagles haunt the skies of bunchgrass prairies on the eastern slopes of the park. — Paul Lally

A

B

C

F

E

D

(A) Thistle. — Gordon Sullivan
(B) Showy Fleabane. — Peter and Alice Bengeyfield
(C) Shooting star. — Peter and Alice Bengeyfield
(D) Yampah. — Gordon Sullivan
(E) Ground squirrel. — Bert Gildart
(F) Pasque Flower. — Bert Gildart

92

By the end of the tenth month, or around the middle of June, snows have receded, and the duration of the sun is at its greatest. Then these tiny structures begin shooting upward, as much as an inch a day in some species.

By the end of July, tiny buds begin to unfurl. And soon these plants, which for a time were drab and difficult to identify, sparkle and assume unique identities. They bounce in the wind, roll across the plains, and tingle as morning zephers waft across their faces. For a brief moment, when measured against the course of a year, they add a multiplicity of colors to the prairie and foothills of the parks.

Yarrow, fleabane, potentilla, cinquefoil, spirea, crazyweed, and lupine are a few of the 1,000 or so species growing in the park. A large percentage of these may be seen in the park's bunchgrass community co-mingling to form this colorful pageantry.

Many of these plants are annuals, or species that produce seeds that must start anew each year. By comparison, perennials sprout each year from roots and produce an annual growth of seeds.

All of the emerging plants serve a vital function in the overall ecological picture. The beneficial effects of some, however, are more readily recognized. Wild geranium is a major food item for elk and deer in spring and summer. At times, this plant is also consumed by black and grizzly bears. It may be recognized by its five rose-purple petals each of which measures about ½ inch across. Stems, leaves and some flower parts are covered with sticky, glandular hairs.

Cinquefoil, which blooms throughout the summer, is used by scientists as an indicator plant. If this plant is being browsed, wildlife biologists know the range is being overgrazed. Because it has five petals and five sepals it is classified as a rose, though it has no thorns.

Yarrow, a plant that produces a white flower, is used medicinally as a stimulant and as a tonic. Indians were familiar with its medicinal applications ages ago. The species generic name, *Achillea*, comes from the Greek hero Achilles, who is supposed to have used yarrow to heal his wounded warriors after the siege of Troy.

In some years, the density of the flowers is greater than in other years. Heavy spring rains followed by an abundance of sunshine may be responsible for this profusion. During these times colors of every hue run up one coulee and down another — running beyond the limits of the imagination as they merge with the sapphire of St. Mary Lake and the aqua of the eastern skies.

Above: Mule deer are abundant in the bunchgrass plant community and range well east of the park toward the prairie. — Bert Gildart
Left: The ever-present coyote in typical bunchgrass ecosystem. — Joe Cerise

Bunchgrass Community

For nine to ten months they lie dormant: Plants that show no flowering life and exist only as seeds, roots, tubers or underground stems. Should you dig one up and look at it all covered with mud, it would appear lifeless; but on the 10th or 11th month transitions begin to occur. Tiny structures begin to emerge known as epicotyls, hypocotyls and cotyledons. These are the predecessors of leaves, roots and the areas of nutrition.

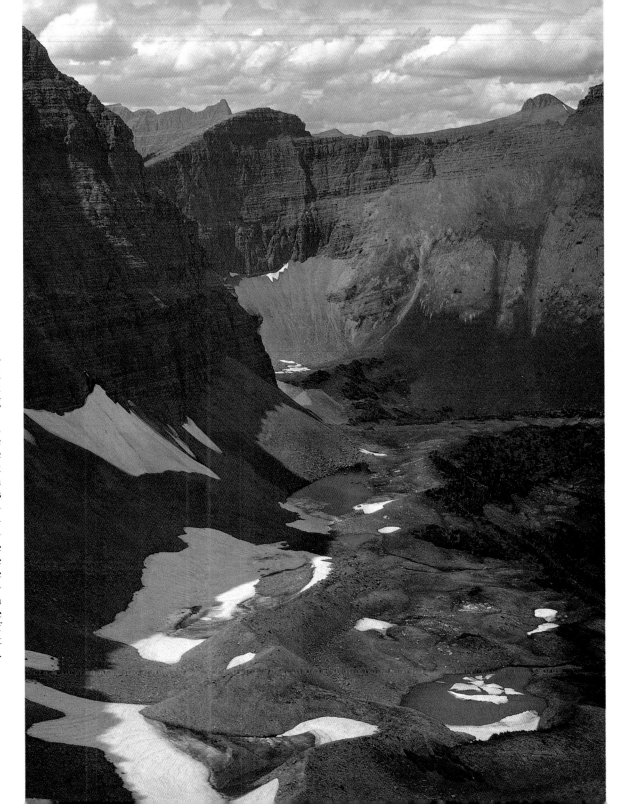

View from Triple Divide Peak to the north. — Bert Gildart

Opposite Page: (A, B, C, E) — Paul Lally
(D) — Bert Gildart

Triple Divide

Of all the mountains in Glacier National Park, Triple Divide Peak is one of the most significant. Rising to an elevation of 8,020 feet it can be easily reached by leaving the ranger station in Cut Bank Valley where a trail leads for approximately eight miles to Triple Divide Pass. From here an hour-long scramble will take you to the summit.

From its apex, waters drain down Atlantic Creek, eventually to reach the Gulf of Mexico. Across the ridge to the left, water flows southwest down Pacific Creek ultimately to mingle with the blue Pacific at the mouth of the Columbia River. To the right, on the other side of the pass, water drains from this peak down Hudson Bay Creek in its course to Hudson Bay. No other peak in North America has drainage into three seas so distant and through watercourses as long as the three river systems: the Missouri-Mississippi, the Columbia, and the Saskatchewan-Nelson. Here is the meeting of the three major divides of North America: the Atlantic-Pacific, the Pacific-Hudson Bay, and the Hudson Bay-Atlantic. But for all of its importance, Triple Divide Peak is not high, since it is only a spur of Norris Mountain to the northwest. The easiest route up the mountain leads directly from the pass. Rock cairns now mark the route.

A

B

C

D

E

Salmon Feast on McDonald Creek

Well after most of the park's annual flow of 1.6 million visitors has streamed through McDonald valley, comes a special group of visitors who have become famous in their own right.

These are the three to six hundred bald eagles that congregate sometime each October or November on a short stretch of McDonald Creek to feast on spawning salmon.

Kokanee salmon, transplanted in Flathead Lake in the early part of the century have sought this stretch of shallow, rapid, waters and its gravelly river bed to mate and die. The resulting feast provides a glimpse of bald eagles in numbers almost hard to imagine to most people, who will never see a single one of these magestic birds.

In a week or two it is all over, the salmon having completed their melancholy cycle, and the eagles move on throughout forests of the Rocky Mountains for the winter.

Biologists are concerned that a parasite on the Kokanee will reduce its numbers or its ability to make the month-long ascent of McDonald Creek and the eagle show will be no more. Even now the Park Service has been forced by concern for the birds to control the sites where the congregation may be viewed.

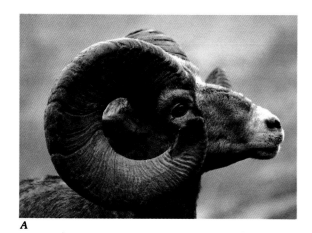

A

Rocky Mountain Bighorn Sheep

Rocky Mountain Bighorn Sheep are almost synonymous with Glacier Park to many visitors because of their visibility in the high-visitor area of Many Glacier. In summer above the historic Many Glacier Hotel, and at other spots such as Haystack Butte, bands of sheep can be seen in seeming peace. But in the mating season of autumn, Many Glacier Valley resounds with cracking blows of horns as males endure annual dominance battles.

B

(A, D) John Winnie, Jr.
(B) Bert Gildart
(C) Tom Ulrich
Opposite Page:
(A) Gordon Sullivan
(B, C) Bert Gildart

C

D

A

B

C

97

A

Mountain Goat

As with the bighorn sheep, there are a few special places where the mountain goat is frequently sought and photographed.

Gunsight Pass is such a place. The classic Glacier Park photos of mountain goats lounging on a rocky outcrop with a jewel of a lake hundreds of feet below likely were taken at Gunsight Pass showing Lake Ellen Wilson in the background. Goats are found throughout the park, but usually are not so easy to find, choosing to live in an environment so remote that they fear little from predators, but suffer instead from the elements and dangers of their craggy homesteads.

(A) Goat above Lake Ellen Wilson. — Bert Gildart
(C, D) Gordon Sullivan photos
Opposite Page
(A, B, C) Bert Gildart

98

C

D

A

C

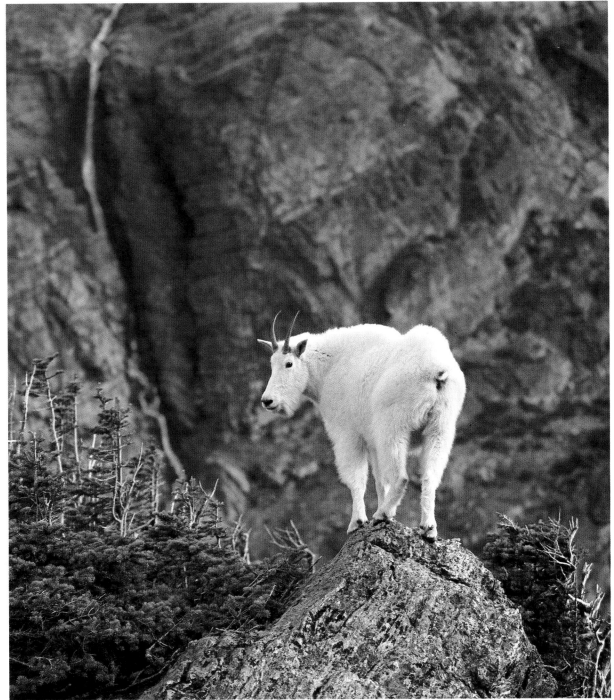

B

A
Spectacular
View
of
Glacier

Courtesy Glacier National Park

1967 oblique aerial photos of Glacier Park looking southeast. The head of Lake McDonald is at the right. Going-to-the-Sun Road can be seen traversing the park and exiting at Saint Mary Lake seen at the extreme upper right corner of the left-hand photo.

Iceberg Lake. — Gordon Sullivan

About Our Back Cover Photo

This photographic mosaic was compiled from Earth Resources Satellite Photo passes made from a height of 570 miles. It was pieced together in black and white and interpreted in color by Big Sky Magic, Larry Dodge, Owner.

Commercial Color Adaptation © 1976 Big Sky Magic.

Front Cover: Left: Lake McDonald, Gordon Sullivan.
Upper Right: Mount Wilbur from Altyn Peak, Peter and Alice Bengeyfield.
Lower Right: On the trail to Iceberg Lake, Gordon Sullivan.
Middle: Mount Reynolds, Rick Graetz.

This series fills the need for in-depth information about Montana subjects. The geographic concept explores the historic color, the huge landscape and the resilient people of a single subject or area. Design by Len Visual Design, Helena, Montana. Color lithography by Dai Nippon, San Francisco. Printed in Hong Kong. All camera prep work and layout production completed in Helena, Montana. Typesetting by Thurber Printing, Helena, Montana.